THE SETTLEMENT OF
CANADIAN–AMERICAN DISPUTES

THE RELATIONS OF
CANADA AND THE UNITED STATES

————

A SERIES OF STUDIES
PREPARED UNDER THE DIRECTION OF THE
CARNEGIE ENDOWMENT FOR INTERNATIONAL PEACE
DIVISION OF ECONOMICS AND HISTORY

JAMES T. SHOTWELL, *Director*

THE
SETTLEMENT
OF
CANADIAN-AMERICAN
DISPUTES

A CRITICAL STUDY
OF METHODS AND RESULTS

BY
P. E. CORBETT, M.C., M.A.

FORMER FELLOW OF ALL SOULS COLLEGE, OXFORD
AND DEAN OF THE FACULTY OF LAW
MᶜGILL UNIVERSITY

NEW YORK / RUSSELL & RUSSELL

FIRST PUBLISHED IN 1937
REISSUED, 1970, BY RUSSELL & RUSSELL
A DIVISION OF ATHENEUM PUBLISHERS, INC.
BY ARRANGEMENT WITH
THE CARNEGIE ENDOWMENT FOR INTERNATIONAL PEACE
L. C. CATALOG CARD NO: 73-102482
PRINTED IN THE UNITED STATES OF AMERICA

PREFACE

In 1932, after preliminary discussions in a group of Americans and Canadians meeting under the genial chairmanship of Dr. J. T. Shotwell, a plan took shape for the impartial, objective study of all the interplay in the activities of our two peoples. The proposed field of work was both long and wide. It stretched far back into the past; its scope embraced all the important points of contact. It was divided roughly among the disciplines of History, Economics, Sociology, Political Science and Law, though everyone concerned knew that the border-lines could not be sharply drawn and that something of all five techniques would probably recur in each division.

Each division was assigned to a group whose members were chosen from Canada and the United States, and the work was sub-divided among these members with due regard to geographical distribution as well as to technical equipment. Much of the task has now reached the publication stage, and a series of volumes is in print or in preparation for the press. For the practical elaboration of the plan, and for its transformation from an idea into a series of concrete studies, we have to thank the Division of Economics and History of the Carnegie Endowment for International Peace and the generosity of the Carnegie Corporation.

Under the heading of Political Science fell studies in (a) the inter-influence of political doctrines and institutions; (b) the establishment of joint organs for the administration of common interests; (c) the administration of justice as between the two nations; and (d) joint legislation in the form of treaties and agreements. The present volume embodies the work done on the third of these subjects. Publications on the others will appear in due course.

Such an essay as this, dealing with the settlement of international disputes, might have been thought to belong exclusively to the field of law. But the processes by which law is formed, the sources of its authority, and the machinery by which it is applied, are all matters which find legitimate place in the science of politics; and the reader who numbers the ordering of the international community among the great tasks of contemporary politics will demand no further explanation. Moreover, though it has been thought necessary to indicate the contributions which the adjudication of Canadian-American disputes has made to international jurisprudence, attention is not concentrated on fine points of law. The book is not designed specially for persons preparing for or engaged in the legal profession; it is aimed at all intelligent students of political and social phenomena, the dominant motive throughout being the common social utility of the methods employed and results achieved in Canadian-American arbitration.

P. E. CORBETT

McGill University
May, 1937

CONTENTS

THE SETTLEMENT OF
CANADIAN-AMERICAN DISPUTES

CHAPTER I

INTRODUCTORY

THERE are probably not two countries in the world under separate sovereignty whose citizens have more closely interwoven interests than those of Canada and the United States or whose national interests are in greater degree common. M. André Siegfried once remarked, in the course of a formal discussion on Canadian-American relations, that the gathering resembled a family party far more than an unofficial international conference. Against his European background, the points of friction with which we were concerned were like the bickerings of close relations in the administration of an inheritance, acrid at times no doubt, but as remote from any possibility of bloodshed as the differences over some delicate partition between fundamentally well-disposed brothers. Moreover, the assimilation in modes of thought and life has proceeded so far that he, along with other competent foreign observers, has predicted political fusion in no very distant future.

We who live here are more chary of prophecy. We know the strong attachment of the average man to certain tenacious differences in political institutions, we know his deep-seated pride each in his own independences, illusory as those may appear under scientific examination. We rate more highly than those who look on from outside the power of these subjective elements to resist the objective reason of the thing. We see no present urge on either side of the border toward union nor any circumstances out of which such an urge is especially likely to develop. On the contrary we note the absence of conditions which in the past have induced minor movements toward annexation, and the growth of factors, particularly in the domain of protected industry, tending to perpetuate our separateness.

That is why political scientists in both countries are studying, not means and modes of assimilation, but means of safeguarding and enhancing what has come to be a traditional understanding between two distinct nations, and at the same time of securing the harmonious advancement of our common interests.

In the history of these two nations there have been many occasions when the acts of one have seemed to the other to constitute a flagrant invasion of this other's peculiar domain, an infringement of its national rights or, at the least, a failure in the qualities of good neighborhood. For more than a hundred years these clashes have not led to war. They have been terminated by negotiation or by arbitral decisions giving compensation where rights were found to have been violated or setting up permanent arrangements for the joint administration or supervision of domains in which conflict was likely to be recurrent.

The record of these adjustments is a treasury of precious experience in the solution of international disputes, and there are several reasons why it has been thought worth-while to compress into small space the essential facts and issues involved in the numerous cases arbitrated, to examine the methods employed in settlement, and to assess the results achieved.

In the first place, universal arbitration is coming to be regarded as a *sine qua non* in any organization for the future peace of the world, and these cases furnish some of the elements from which a consistent jurisprudence may be built up for the guidance of arbiters. In recent years politicians from North America have displayed in European conferences a complacency which has sometimes approached the offensive on the score of our long record of peaceful and rational relations. There is of course reason for satisfaction in our "century of peace and three thousand miles of undefended frontier"; but only those derive a feeling of superiority from these circumstances who forget, or never knew, how narrow the margin has sometimes been between peace and war, and who fail to give credit to the special advantages with which we began our career of neighborhood.

Between Great Britain and the United States there has always been a strong pre-disposition to peace. The Republic owes its separate existence to a civil war in which the thirteen colonies attained their objective because they were, on the whole, a little less half-hearted than the mother country. In the one violent conflict which has interrupted their normal relations from 1783 to the present time, the only intensely earnest and whole-hearted element was the Canadian population, who enjoyed the incalculable inspiration of defending their homes against an invader.

Blood is no sure guaranty against bloodshed; but when community of race is reënforced by a mercantile spirit acutely conscious of mutual economic usefulness, there is bound to be a powerful prejudice against the dislocation of war. The original identity and continued similarity of legal systems, coupled with confidence on both sides in the common judicial process, add another motive for resort, not to force, but to investigation and adjudication.

Bearing in mind these premises, we can understand the very remarkable record of conciliation and arbitration between Great Britain or Canada and the United States. The range of subject matter with which it has been found possible to deal by diplomatic, judicial, or semijudicial methods includes the definition and demarcation of a boundary through some thousands of miles of imperfectly mapped territory, a process which has taken a century and a half to complete, and which involved the determination of sovereignty in disputed areas of large extent; rights of fishery in Atlantic and Pacific coastal waters; pollution, obstruction, navigation and power development in hundreds of miles of boundary rivers and lakes; aërial navigation and radio broadcasting; and, finally, that inexhaustible source of friction between nations—injuries to the persons and property of citizens. In many specific cases of conflict falling under these general headings, popular feeling on both sides has been roused to the danger point, and loud expression has been given to views of "vital interest" and "national honor." There have repeatedly been present all the elements which have brought sudden and bitter war between peoples less charitably disposed. The facts are an eloquent challenge to the validity of the doctrine, still stoutly maintained in many quarters, that there are disputes in which, owing either to the nature of the issue, or to the circumstances in which it presents itself, the State can only be true to itself by remaining its own judge. For, though many of the compromises accepted and many of the decisions rendered have inevitably aroused vituperative indignation on one side or the other, there is little reason to believe that the habit of peaceful settlement has crippled the development of either country concerned, or weakened the morale of its population.

Such is the claim of our material to general attention. That its importance has not been unappreciated by the specialists must be evident to readers of treatises on international law, where arbitrations like those on the fur seals of the Behring Sea and the North Atlantic fisheries take prominent place among *causes célèbres*. But the full story has a value not to be comprehended from isolated episodes.

The full story is an essential part in the history of the settlement and civilization of North America. Clearly those adjustments which have been attempted in other parts of the world by war, with its untold suffering and its unjust and temporary results, have been achieved here by peaceful means with comparative ease, with reasonable permanency, and, if not always with ideal equity, at least with a much closer approach thereto than could be expected from any arbitrament of arms. That is the strongest appeal of this record to the particular attention of North Americans; and it is matter for some astonishment that so little space has been devoted to the subject in our histories, and that the fragmentary mentions of the more spectacular issues so often display an animus which distorts facts and disregards significant achievement.

With this intellectual interest there is joined some measure of practical utility. Inevitably, between countries situated as we are, there will be irritations in the future as there have been in the past. More widespread and accurate knowledge of the way in which the multifarious disputes of a century and a quarter have been settled will bring a calmer attitude at times when national views of right and obligation clash. This is an aspect of our study which has a special importance for Canadians, who are still prone to assume that we have invariably lost in our litigations with the United States and accordingly that no confidence in ultimate justice can be entertained when our interests come into conflict with theirs. The following pages present neither the American nor the Canadian as a self-sacrificing altruist. There is keen trading and clever advocacy on both sides: the record is no story of wolf and lamb.

NARROWLY interpreted, Canadian-American disputes would include only those in which Canada appears directly as the antagonist of the United States. If its scope were so limited, this study would have to begin with the very recent emergence of Canada as a distinct member of the community of nations, stretching a point perhaps to cover the work of the International Joint Commission set up in 1910. In so doing, we should omit all consideration of some of the most significant arbitrations in the whole history of international politics and ignore the deep roots of the tradition of adjudication now so firmly established between these neighbor countries. The term used in our title must therefore be understood to comprise all the conflicts between the British Crown and the United States which have been primarily concerned with the territorial or other interests of Canada. Our point of departure must accordingly lie not far from 1783, when the Treaty of Paris recognized the independence of the new Republic.

From 1783 to 1794 the burning issues were mainly those left un-settled by the Treaty of Paris. They had to do with the division of territory, compensation for slaves carried off in the course of hostili-ties, and the payment of pre-revolutionary debts owing by citizens of the revolting colonies to continuing British subjects. It was fortu-nate that throughout this period Hamilton and the Federalists, the dominant group in the formation of policy, insisted that the Ameri-can nation must have peace in which to develop unity and strength. After 1788 the Federal Government was dependent for its resources on the revenue derived from trade with Great Britain, and Hamil-ton's dearest wish was to avoid the dislocation which war would bring to this commerce. Thus it came about that the cynical refusal of Great Britain to deliver up the fur-trading posts within American territory, on the ostensible ground of American violation of the treaty in its debt-repayment clauses, did not result in a renewal of hostilities.

In the negotiations leading to the Jay Treaty of 1794, the Ameri-can demand of compensation for negroes carried off and freed by the British forces was dropped. The treaty itself made new provision for the surrender of the posts and these were in fact handed over in 1796. Having disposed of this *bête noire*, the treaty went on to set up commissions to deal with the other matters in dispute between the parties. One of these commissions dealt successfully with the claims of American subjects for damages suffered by the capture of their ships and merchandise by British cruisers in the Anglo-French war, and with the claims of British subjects based on the capture of vessels and goods by the French within the jurisdiction of the United States. Another, charged with the settlement of the dispute about debts owing to British subjects, broke up in disagreement, leaving the matter to be disposed of by diplomatic negotiation and the payment, by the American Government, of $2,664,000.

For the purposes of the present study, Jay's Treaty is interesting for two reasons, one general and the other particular. The general reason is that it initiated the practice of peaceful settlement between the British Empire and the United States: the particular reason is that it began the long process of defining, by joint commissions, the Canadian-American boundary.

This monograph will attempt to provide in the next four chapters a condensed version of the whole history of Canadian-American conciliation and arbitration proceedings. In setting about this task, there is a choice of two methods. One may adopt a purely chronological order, or break the record up into sections according to subject matter. The latter course has been chosen, and the headings are as follows: 1. Settlement of the boundary; 2. Fisheries; 3. Inland waterways; 4. Miscellaneous claims.

When the narrative is completed, we shall be in a position to evaluate certain specific contributions which these proceedings have brought into the fund of rules or principles that guide international tribunals. We shall also be able to judge, in the light of a prolonged practice, how far the machinery employed meets the needs of the present, and by what changes or additions it might be made to operate more smoothly and efficiently. Our concluding chapters will be devoted to these questions.

CHAPTER II

SETTLEMENT OF THE BOUNDARY

THE ST. CROIX RIVER, 1798

ARTICLE V of Jay's Treaty established the first of the many commissions which have labored in the definition of our famous three-thousand-mile frontier. Its business was to decide what stream was intended under the name of the river St. Croix mentioned in the Treaty of Paris, 1783, as part of the line between what are now respectively the State of Maine and the Province of New Brunswick.

The well-directed industry of this commission, the urbanity which marked its proceedings, and the success to which these qualities led, made it something of a model and are factors of cardinal importance in determining the general trend of Canadian-American relations. That is why I devote to its work a space which is perhaps out of proportion to the interest at stake.

One commissioner was to be named by Great Britain, one by the United States. The two were to choose a third, either by agreement, or, if they could not agree, by drawing lots between their respective nominees. The first choice of the President of the United States fell upon General Knox; but he declined to act

on the ground, among others, that he had a personal interest in the result of the controversy.[1]

David Howell, a lawyer from Rhode Island, was accordingly appointed. Great Britain chose Thomas Barclay, also a lawyer, a United Empire loyalist settled at Annapolis in Nova Scotia.

These two gentlemen agreed, without recourse to lot, upon Egbert Benson a third lawyer, from New York. He, though a cousin of Barclay, had been suggested by Howell. The circumstance is mentioned as indicating the frank and friendly spirit in which the commission's task was approached.

1. Quoted in John Bassett Moore, *History and Digest of the International Arbitrations to Which the United States Has Been a Party* (Washington, Government Printing Office, 1898), I, 6.

After professional surveys, personal examination of the locality, and a study of all relevant evidence, including the records of the French discoverers, the commissioners found in favor of the British contention that the true St. Croix was what was commonly called the Schoodiac, and not the more easterly Magaguadavic. The St. Croix branched some distance above its mouth, and there remained to be decided which of these branches, traced to its source, was intended as the boundary. The definition of the source had a further significance: from it was to be drawn a line due north to

the Highlands which divide those rivers that empty themselves into the River St. Lawrence, from those which fall into the Atlantic Ocean[2]

—simple words that enfolded a conflict destined to drag on, with threats of armed violence, until 1842. But this line and its conflict were no part of the business of the St. Croix Commission, whose labors terminated with the location of the source. Here the commission adopted the view of Mr. Howell, the American appointee, selecting the northerly rather than the westerly branch and marking the source with "a stake near a Yellow Birch Tree, hooped with iron."[3] The unanimous declaration of the commissioners was issued on October 25, 1798, two and a half years after their appointment.

In his report to the President of the United States, Benson freely admitted that compromise served as the basis of decision in the second part of the commission's task. The language which he used states simply but clearly an eternal principle of successful international conciliation and adjustment:

the reference, as it respected the source of the River, being as it were an appeal to mere judgment or opinion, is in that view analogous to cases of assessment of damages not capable of being liquidated by *calculation,* or *definite* Rule, and therefore to be assessed according to discernment, or discretion; a latitude of arbitrament is in such cases supposed to be permitted to the Jurors, but as they must at the same time agree in a precise sum, accommodation of sentiment among them to a degree is necessary, and consequently justifiable.[4]

2. Treaty of Paris, 1783, Art. 2.
3. Declaration of the Commissioners, Moore, *op. cit.,* p. 30.
4. Moore, *op. cit.,* p. 42.

THE PASSAMAQUODDY ISLANDS, 1817

THE same willingness to compromise where no conclusive ground of decision offered enabled the commission of two persons set up under Article IV of the Treaty of Ghent, 1814, to reach a rapid division of the islands in the bays of Passamaquoddy and Fundy. The Treaty of Paris had assigned these islands to the United States, except such as were situated within the limits of Nova Scotia. In order to decide upon the scope of this exception, the commissioners were thrown back upon the original grant of the area to Sir William Alexander in 1631 and the subsequent commissions issued to British governors. These documents differed in wording and were susceptible of varied interpretations. The British Commissioner was again Thomas Barclay, and he was particularly anxious to secure Grand Manan for his country. The assent of the American Commissioner, Mr. Holmes, was perhaps hastened by the fact that he had just been elected to Congress and desired to complete his task before that body assembled. On November 24, 1817, just fourteen months after their first meeting, Messrs. Barclay and Holmes issued their decision assigning Moose, Dudley, and Frederick islands to the United States, and all the others, including Grand Manan, to His Britannic Majesty. Grand Manan remained something of a sore spot with the United States, but the finding was loyally accepted.

THE NORTHEASTERN FRONTIER, 1816–1842

ARTICLE V of the same Treaty of Ghent provided for a commission of two persons to deal with the vexed question of the northeastern frontier. The Treaty of Paris, 1783, had taken as the starting point of the east and west boundary

the northwest angle of Nova Scotia, viz. that angle which is formed by a line drawn due north from the source of the Saint Croix River to the Highlands. . . .

Thence the line was to follow

the said Highlands which divide those rivers that empty themselves into the river St. Lawrence, from those which fall into the Atlantic Ocean, to the northwesternmost head of the Connecticut River; thence down along the middle of that river, to the 45th degree of north latitude; from thence, by a line due west on said latitude until it strikes the River Iroquois or Cataraquy. . . .

Unfortunately there was no mountainous ridge in the area, and the possibilities as to the situation of the "angle" were therefore almost unlimited.

Thomas Barclay was again appointed by Great Britain, but this time he found his American colleague less pliable. They met from time to time between September, 1816, and October, 1824, studied the results of elaborate surveys, listened to argument by the agents of the two Governments, and broke up in hopeless disagreement.

The Treaty of Ghent had provided not for a third commissioner so that there might be a majority decision, but for reference, in case of disagreement between the two commissioners, to a friendly sovereign or state. In 1828 the King of the Netherlands was chosen and consented to act. His award was issued in 1831. He had decided that the "highlands" claimed respectively by the United States and Great Britain as forming, with the line from the source of the St. Croix the "northwest angle" of Nova Scotia, were about equally remote from satisfying the description in the treaty. The surveys had revealed no satisfactory intermediate highlands, and the King was left with the dilemma of declaring the problem insoluble or drawing frankly a compromise line. He chose the latter alternative, giving out of a total disputed territory of 12,027 square miles 4,119 square miles to Great Britain and 7,908 to the United States.

Great Britain accepted the award without question, but the American Senate voted by a large majority for its rejection. In the event, this rejection proved slightly worse than useless, but there was some legal ground for it. The King of the Netherlands had been asked to investigate and make a decision upon the points of difference between the parties. Their difference was as to the meaning of the treaty of 1783 and the arbiter had simply abandoned the attempt to find out what the meaning was, substituting for the boundary described in that instrument one which, for a large portion of its course, ignored all question of "highlands" and "northwest corners." Then followed ten years of sporadic negotiation, new suggestions of a boundary from both sides, new surveys, and unpleasant border incidents. Happily the "Restook War," an imbroglio of lumbermen and officials from New Brunswick and Maine, resulted in no casualties. British-American relations had been further embittered by the *Caroline* incident at Niagara in 1838 and its sequels; and the population in both countries was aroused to a point where any actual bloodshed might well have meant real war. There has been no small element of sheer luck in our hundred and twenty years of official peace.

Such was the very anxious condition of affairs when Daniel Webster, who became Secretary of State in 1841, cut through the tangled mass of proposals and counter-proposals with a new offer to try for a settlement by direct negotiation between fully authorized representatives of the British and American Governments. The result was the Ashburton-Webster Treaty of 1842.

The line accepted by Lord Ashburton and Mr. Webster was a diplomatic compromise rather than an agreed interpretation of the treaty of 1783. It gave to Canada 893 square miles more than the King of the Netherlands had assigned to her, and that was the net American loss from the Senate's rejection of the royal award.

The settlement was subjected to savage attacks on both sides of the Atlantic. The Senate's consent was only induced by Webster's use of the famous "red-line" map. This, which, it was feared, might be the map on which Benjamin Franklin, as peace commissioner in Paris in 1782–1783, had marked the limits claimed by the colonies, gave to Great Britain far more than the Ashburton-Webster agreement. It had not been revealed in the negotiations; but if this was duplicity it was matched by the fact that the British Government was at the same time secreting the map used by Oswald as British delegate to the peace conference, a map very injurious to the case argued by Lord Ashburton in 1842.

Lord Ashburton's American wife, and his known friendliness toward the United States, were the burden of attacks at Westminster. In fact they were important contributors to his success in a difficult task. Webster's breadth of mind and direct methods, held responsible in his own country for the surrender of American "rights," were nothing more than a sensible man's reaction against the mixture of intransigence and pettifoggery which for half a century had kept the northeastern boundary a suppurating sore in British-American relations.

To this day the settlement is occasionally mentioned in Canada as one of the outstanding instances where Canadian interests have been sacrificed by the Mother Country to her own purposes, and as evidence of the alleged futility of expecting justice in disputes with the United States. Yet it is more than manifest to the objective observer at this distance of time that a reasonable compromise, such as that actually adopted, was the only possible way out of the uncertainties and contradictions of one of history's most complex boundary disputes. The settlement is one more demonstration of the tremendous effect of reasonableness and geniality, without weakness, in the persons engaged. Finally, there is one simple consideration which goes a long way to deprive the Canadian grievance of any justification; it is that the Ashburton-Webster division actually gave more to Canada than it had received under the award of an arbiter whose impartiality was never in question.

ST. LAWRENCE TO LAKE SUPERIOR, 1842

WEBSTER and Ashburton were able in their treaty to dispose of another difference which, because smaller tracts of territory were involved and because this territory was still almost uninhabited, had not occasioned any bitterness. Article VI and VII of the Treaty of Ghent had set up yet another commission of one American and one British subject to "fix and determine" the boundary from St. Regis, where the forty-fifth degree of north latitude intersects the St. Lawrence River, through the whole chain of rivers and lakes to the northwesternmost point of the Lake of the Woods, determining at the same time to which side the numerous islands in this great waterway belonged. This commission had gone quietly about its work and by December, 1827, had struck off an agreed line except at two points. It had been forced to record disagreement as to which of the channels about St. George's Island, in St. Mary's River between Lakes Huron and Superior, should form the boundary. The sovereignty of St. George's Island, some forty square miles in area, was thus left in doubt. The two commissioners had also parted company between the western end of Lake Superior and Lac la Pluie, which lies about two thirds of the way along to the Lake of the Woods.

Now Articles VI and VII of the Treaty of Ghent had made the

same provision as Articles IV and V for the event of disagreement
on the part of the commissioners, namely, that recourse should then
be had to the arbitration of a friendly sovereign or state. But such
was the preoccupation of the contending parties with the Maine
border that no move to carry this arrangement into effect was made
on either side. Accordingly the two points were still in dispute when
Ashburton and Webster met in 1842.

Ashburton conceded St. George's Island in return for navigation
privileges through the American channels in Lake St. Clair and
about Long Sault and Barnhart islands. As for the line from Isle
Royale, at the west end of Lake Superior, to Lac la Pluie, he made
no attempt to support the extreme claim maintained by the British
Commissioner in 1827, which would have brought the boundary near
what is now Duluth, but proposed instead the compromise line which
the American Commissioner, probably because it was linked with the
surrender of St. George's Island, had at that date refused. He
finally agreed with Webster on the Pigeon River, about six miles
farther north. Their decision involved the sacrifice of some six thousand square miles previously claimed by the United States. But in
abandoning the extreme British claim, the British Commissioner in
1827 and Ashburton in 1842 were giving up a much larger area of
what seemed at the time almost valueless territory. It is one of the
small ironies of history that this area would appear, from a study of
the available maps, to contain the vast Mesabi and Vermilion iron
deposits. If the existence of these deposits had been known in 1842,
the division would have been infinitely more difficult and would have
called for concessions that might have materially altered the course
of the boundary at other points as well. As it was, the decision on
Lake Superior, which in the event has separated Ontario from iron
mines that would have added greatly to the wealth of the Dominion,
passed with little notice; while Canadian indignation concentrated
on imaginary losses to New Brunswick and Quebec.

It had been assumed in the treaty of 1783 that a line due west
from the most northwestern point of the Lake of the Woods would
intersect the Mississippi, and this line was to be the east and west
boundary in this region. Subsequent surveys showed that the sources
of the Mississippi were all to the south of the Lake of the Woods,
and a new scheme of division had therefore to be adopted. In 1803,

France ceded Louisiana to the United States, and in negotiations with Great Britain after this date, the American Government argued that the northern limit of Louisiana was the forty-ninth parallel, which figured in the Treaty of Utrecht, 1713, as the southern limit of the Hudson Bay Company's territories. This contention was never firmly opposed by Great Britain, though the Treaty of Utrecht had not purported to define the boundary between Canada and Louisiana, and a more natural division would have been along the watershed of the Mississippi and Missouri. By 1814 all that the British Government asked was the right of navigation in the Mississippi. The American delegation at Ghent refused this; and in 1818 the Convention of Commerce laid it down that the line of demarcation to the Rocky Mountains should be

drawn from the most northwesternmost point of the Lake of the Woods, along the 49th parallel . . . or, if the said point shall not be in the 49th parallel . . . then . . . from the said point due north or south, as the case may be, until the said line shall intersect the said parallel . . . and from the point of such intersection due west along and with the said parallel. . . .

The most northwestern point of the Lake of the Woods was determined and marked between 1822 and 1827 by the two commissioners carrying out Article VII of the Treaty of Ghent, and it was their decision, in conjunction with the above Article II of the convention of 1818, that brought about the curious jog in our boundary which has so irritated certain Canadian historians.[5] The Ashburton-Webster Treaty of 1842 merely adopted the findings of the aforementioned commission.

OREGON, 1846

WHEN the above Convention of Commerce was being drafted in 1818, the American negotiators proposed that the forty-ninth parallel should be carried through as the boundary to the Pacific Ocean. Great Britain, however, asserted her right to all the territory north and west of the Columbia River. The country was almost empty of settlements, its sole use being as a source of furs, and there was no

5. For example William Kingsford, who numbers this among the iniquities of Lord Ashburton. See his *History of Canada* (Toronto, 1894), VII, 183.

urgent necessity for immediate delimitation. The parties accordingly agreed that all this territory on the northwest coast of America beyond the Rocky Mountains should be free and open to the nationals of both for a term of ten years. This agreement, which was

not to be construed to the prejudice of any claim which either party might have to any part of the said Country,

was included in the convention as Article III.

From time to time during the ten-year period of this convention, attempts were made to arrive at an agreed division. The United States, however, clung to the forty-ninth parallel as their ultimate concession; while Great Britain refused to settle in these terms on the general ground that she was entitled to everything down to the mouth of the Columbia, and for the special reason that the forty-ninth parallel cut off the south end of Vancouver Island. By 1827 it was evident that the best that could be done was to renew the convention of 1818, with a proviso for denunciation with twelve months' notice.

Extremists in the United States insisted that the whole of the coast and the whole of the Columbia basin up to the southern boundary of Russia at 54° 40′ belonged to their country. Their case rested on (1) the cession of Louisiana, with its indefinite western extension, in 1803; (2) the Treaty of Florida Blanca, whereby in 1819 Spain had surrendered to the United States all her territory on the west coast from 42° northward; (3) the explorations of the American citizens Gray, Lewis, and Clark between 1792 and 1806; and (4) the establishment of trading posts.

In 1844 the Democratic convention adopted among the planks of its platform a declaration that the title to the whole Oregon territory was "clear and unquestionable," and that no part thereof should be ceded. It was this item in the party program which became the delightfully alliterative election slogan, "Fifty-four forty or fight," and President Polk entered on office in 1845 with loud determination to make good this pledge.

Two months before Polk's inauguration, and again in December, 1845, the British Government proposed arbitration; but both offers were rejected. Great Britain founded her title on (1) Drake's explorations in 1579, which had extended along the Pacific coast as far as 48° N. with a landing at Bodega Bay and a formal taking of possession of this "New Albion" in the Queen's name; (2) Cook's survey of the coast from 47° N. to the Arctic in 1776; (3) the visit of an expedition under Lt. John Meares of the Royal Navy to the estuary of the Columbia in 1788, followed by that of Vancouver in 1792; and (4) exploration of the river for 100 miles by Broughton, of Vancouver's expedition, and his formal taking of possession.

In their evidence of title by discovery and possession, both sides were pitifully weak. Spanish, British, and American explorations had all equally failed to be followed by that effective occupation which alone gives sovereignty. Neither in their own right, nor in the right derived from Spain, could the Americans show anything more real by way of occupation than the establishment, in 1811, by the Pacific Fur Company, of Fort Astoria at the mouth of the Columbia. Against this the British cited four posts built by the North-West Company south of 49° N. between 1808 and 1810. As for the immigration of American settlers between 1841 and 1845, these newcomers would have starved but for the relief provided by officials of the Hudson Bay Company; and in any case such settlement as they had effected had been accomplished under the condominium agreement renewed in 1827 and could not therefore prejudice the question of sovereignty.

The whole matter was eminently one for reasonable and friendly arrangement. Had it gone to arbitration, it is difficult to conceive how the arbitrator could have done anything but propose, as the King of Holland had done in the Maine boundary dispute, a division based upon equity rather than strict right. These truths must have been apparent to anyone reflecting calmly on the situation, and most of the bitterness which accumulated in 1844 and 1845 sprang from the malicious folly of making an election issue of so doubtful a question. The grave menace of war which formed the climax demonstrates the danger of carrying a delicate problem of diplomacy into the arena of party politics.

To James Buchanan, Secretary of State, belongs much credit for his eagerness to continue negotiations, rather than sharpen the controversy by such unqualified assertions of right as President Polk continued to indulge in until the end of 1845. In July he persuaded the President to offer again the forty-ninth parallel—a large retrogression from 50° 40′—this time with freedom of any ports on Vancouver Island south of that line. The British Minister at Washington, Richard Pakenham, somewhat brusquely and without consulting his Government, refused to consider this severance of the Island; and Polk, offended, was for abandoning the attempt at compromise. It was not until McLane, American Minister in London, reported that Great Britain was seriously preparing for war, that the President signified readiness to renew discussion.

With this new impetus, Buchanan and Pakenham were able to agree upon the treaty of 1846. This carries the boundary from the Rocky Mountains along the forty-ninth parallel

to the middle of the channel which separates the continent from Vancouver's Island; and thence southerly, through the middle of the said channel, and of Fuca's Straits to the Pacific Ocean.

Thus was the whole of Vancouver Island finally assigned to Great Britain, who in addition obtained for her subjects the right to navigate the Columbia. The treaty also, following the salutary principle of the Ashburton-Webster settlement, declared free and open to both parties the navigation of the channels through which the dividing line runs.

JUAN DE FUCA, 1872

THE boundary was not yet finished. The language quoted above from the Treaty of 1846 was ambiguous, because there were two main channels either of which might be described as separating "the continent from Vancouver's Island." These were the Canal de Haro and Rosario Strait. Upon the answer to the question which of these had been intended by the treaty, depended the sovereignty of a number of islands which in the fifties were attracting attention as desirable sites for settlement. In 1854 the newly created legislature of Washington Territory incorporated San Juan Island in one of its counties.

It thus became desirable to define the boundary on the spot. In 1856–1857 a joint commission was appointed for this purpose. It held six meetings, but in December, 1857, had to admit final disagreement. The British Commissioner had offered to compromise on a line passing between Orcas, Shaw, and Lopez islands on the east, and San Juan Island on the west. This would have left San Juan to Great Britain, and the American Commissioner had flatly refused.

In 1859 there were twenty-five American families and a Hudson's Bay sheep station on San Juan. One of the Americans, charged with shooting a pig belonging to the station, reported that an officer of the company had threatened to arrest and take him to Victoria for trial. General Harney, commanding American troops in Oregon, occupied the island with a small force designed to prevent British interference with the American settlers. Following a protest by Great Britain, arrangements were made for joint military occupation.

In the next ten years, the British Government twice attempted to have the question settled by arbitration. On the second occasion, in 1869, a convention was actually drawn up submitting it to the President of the Swiss Confederation, who was to determine the intention of the Oregon Treaty or, if this proved impossible, to define what would be an equitable boundary. This laudable effort, which would have given to the arbitrator powers which in 1837 the King of the Netherlands had assumed, only to have his decision rejected by the American Senate, was defeated in advance by the same body.

Finally, it was agreed in Article 34 of the Treaty of Washington, 1871, that the Emperor of Germany should be asked to decide which of the two claims, Canal de Haro or Rosario Strait, was

most in accordance with the true interpretation of the treaty of June 15, 1846.

The strong point in the American case was that, as the deflection from the forty-ninth parallel was conceded in 1846 solely for the purpose of leaving Vancouver Island intact, the deflection should be the smallest that would secure this result. They had no difficulty in showing from the correspondence that the main consideration in the minds of the British statesmen involved had been to avoid an awkward division of territory.

Great Britain argued that the channel mentioned in the treaty could be none other than that which had been most accurately explored and charted and was most used at the time. This was undoubtedly Rosario Strait. Further, the Canal de Haro did not separate Vancouver Island from the mainland, but only from a scattered group of islands. Relatively, the case was weak, and the readiness shown by Great Britain, throughout the protracted negotiations, to compromise, was probably due to consciousness of this fact rather than to any superior magnanimity.

After a report from three eminent jurists, William I decided categorically in favor of the United States.

ALASKA, 1903

FROM time to time after 1867, when Russia ceded her North American territory to the United States, the British and American Governments in turn opened the question of a joint commission to define the boundary between Alaska and Canada. The line adopted in the treaty of 1825 between Russia and Great Britain was altogether too vague for practical purposes. Beyond a provisional definition at certain strategic points such as the intersection with the Stikine River, however, little progress had been achieved before the Klondike gold rush of the late Nineties, and the ensuing importance of the waterways, ports, and passes giving entry to the new Eldorado, made the decision of sovereignty a matter of urgent concern.

The Joint High Commission of 1898–1899 was expected to solve this knotty problem among many others, but failed to do so. A *modus vivendi* was, however, agreed upon in 1899, and in 1903 a convention concluded at Washington made provision for a final judicial settlement of the points in dispute.

The tribunal was to consist of "six impartial jurists of repute, who shall consider judicially the questions submitted to them," three being appointed by His Britannic Majesty and three by the President of the United States. So runs Article I of the convention of January 24, 1903; and the words "impartial" and "judicially" were destined, as will be seen, to play a rôle of great importance.

The questions which the tribunal was called upon to "answer and decide" were set out in Article IV. They were seven in number and they all turned upon the meaning of the Anglo-Russian Treaty of 1825, which purported to define the boundary between the British and Russian possessions in North America. In several instances the answers to these questions merged, and the difficulties which the "six impartial jurists" had to solve all centered about the following points:

1. What channel is the Portland Channel?

2. Was it the intention of the treaty of 1825 to give to Russia a strip, of not more than ten marine leagues, following the sinuosities of the coast in such a way as to separate the British possessions from the bays, ports, and inlets, or only a strip following the general direction of the mainland coast and intersecting the longer inlets?

3. What, if any exist, are the mountains parallel to the coast which, when within ten marine leagues from the coast, are declared in the treaty of 1825 to form the eastern boundary?

By a majority of four to two, the tribunal defined the Portland Channel as that passing to the north of Pierce and Wales islands and then turning almost at right angles to enter the ocean between Wales Island on the east and Sitklan Island on the west. The dissenting members were the two Canadians, Sir Louis Jetté and Mr. A. B. Aylesworth. In their written opinions these gentlemen maintain, with rather compelling logic, that in making this deflection, instead of following the Channel straight out to sea between Kannaghunut Island on the south and Tongas Island on the north, the tribunal was compromising "the plain facts of the case" and following a procedure which, far from being "judicial," as the convention of 1903 demanded, was a "grotesque travesty of justice."[6]

Their practical reason for objecting to the decision strikes the present-day reader as somewhat unsubstantial. The tribunal's majority finding gave to the United States Sitklan and Kannaghunut islands, which Mr. Aylesworth describes as being

of the utmost consequence, for they lie directly opposite to, and command the entrance to, the very important harbour of Port Simpson, British Columbia.

It is to be hoped that, in any controversies which may in future arise between Canada and the United States, the strategic value of minute islands will not weigh so heavily. Probably the consideration of our relations in terms of the military defense of one country against the other may be regarded as a thing of the past.

It is not, however, any conceivable military value of these islets which has preserved in Canada a bitter memory of the Alaskan boundary dispute. Indignation at once concentrated upon what was

6. From the opinion of A. B. Aylesworth, K.C., quoted in *Alaskan Boundary Tribunal* (Washington, Government Printing Office), I, 86–87.

felt to be a political compromise rather than a judicial decision on the part of Lord Alverstone, when he acceded to the American claim in this particular. The Lord Chief Justice was accused of handing over the islands to satisfy the American members' anxiety for a diplomatic victory and to prevent them rejecting the whole decision.[7] Such a course, very justifiable at a pinch in any process of conciliation or diplomatic negotiation, was held to be totally out of keeping with the judicial nature of the tribunal as it is explicitly described in the convention of reference. It confirmed the criticism leveled by so many Canadians at President Roosevelt when he chose, as two of his "impartial jurists," Senators Lodge and Turner, of whom the first had already taken a public and categorical stand against the Canadian claims, while the second represented in Congress the State, Washington, most interested in the success of the American case.[8]

In the answer to Question 2 above, Lord Alverstone again took sides with the American jurists, making a majority of four against the two Canadian members of the tribunal. But in this instance his Lordship's decision was by no means so fantastic as when he diverted the Portland Channel. He states that after careful search he had found no evidence that Great Britain had put forward any claim in the negotiations of 1825 to the shores or ports at the head of the inlets.[9] The treaty in which those negotiations resulted took as the eastern boundary, for the purposes of its fourth article,

a line parallel to the windings of the coast, and which shall never exceed the distance of ten marine leagues therefrom;

and the Lord Chief Justice rejected the British contention that this meant only the windings of the general coast, excluding inlets. In spite of the learned reasoning of Sir Louis Jetté and Mr. Aylesworth, I cannot regard as unreasonable the view that "windings of the coast" was intended to include all the recesses filled by salt water.

To some extent the decision on Question 3 above depended upon the answer to Question 2. The tribunal, having by a majority found

7. See, for example, James White, in *Canada and Its Provinces* (Toronto, 1914), VIII, 940–941.

8. See Hugh Ll. Keenleyside, *Canada and the United States* (New York, 1929), pp. 218–219, quoting the Ottawa *Citizen* of February 23, 1903.

9. *Alaskan Boundary Tribunal,* I, 40.

that Russia had intended to retain a strip of territory around the heads of all inlets, could not take a line of mountains that cut across them. There was in fact no range with anything in the nature of a continuous crest close to the coast, but the British argument, accepted by Sir Louis Jetté and Mr. Aylesworth, contended that the treaty of 1825 had reference to the isolated mountains, sometimes within a few miles of the coast, whose summits could be joined by an imaginary line to form the boundary. The majority, having taken the view it did on Question 2 above, felt constrained to look much farther inland, and the line of mountain peaks which it used for a long stretch of the boundary lies for the most part about thirty miles from the coast.

The whole decision proved a source of lasting dissatisfaction in Canada. It is safe to conclude, however, that for much the greater part this discontent was attributable to extrinsic elements of the case rather than to the fact of defeat. The truculent attitude of President Roosevelt, the choice of the American members of the tribunal,[10] the not unreasonable suspicion that Lord Alverstone's opinions had been swayed by a diplomatic motive, these were the things that were featured by the Canadian press and that continued to smart in the Canadian mind. To a very considerable degree such impediments to confidence in the judicial solution of differences between nations can be avoided by arbitration conventions drawn up, not for any specific dispute but to operate in the event of dispute, particularly if such conventions provide for the selection of arbiters from a previously established panel, or, better still, from persons not nationals of the litigants. It is interesting to note that when, in 1908, a treaty was concluded for

the more complete definition and demarcation of the international boundary between the United States and the Dominion of Canada,

a treaty intended to dispose of minor uncertainties and to provide for re-monumentation along the whole line from Passamaquoddy Bay to the Pacific Ocean, arrangements were included for the arbi-

10. Keenleyside, *op. cit.,* pp. 219–221, quoting *Springfield Republican,* February 23, 1903. For President Roosevelt's letter to Judge Holmes, July 25, 1903, see Bishop, *Theodore Roosevelt and His Time Shown in His Own Letters* (New York, 1920), I, 259–261.

tration of possible differences by a tribunal of non-partisan character. It may be assumed that the memory of 1903 was in the minds of the negotiators when they drafted the careful terms of Articles I and II. Any difference between boundary commissioners which the Governments fail to settle within six months by direct negotiation is to be referred to

an arbitrator to ve agreed upon by the two Governments, or, in case of a failure to agree, to be appointed by a third Power selected by the two Governments by common accord, or, if no agreement is thus arrived at, each Government shall select a different Power and the choice of the arbitrator shall be made in concert by the Powers thus selected.[11]

11. *Treaties and Agreements Affecting Canada in Force between His Majesty and the United States of America, with Subsidiary Documents, 1814–1925* (Ottawa, F. A. Acland, 1927), pp. 301–303.

CHAPTER III

FISHERIES

THE Treaty of Paris of 1783, which established peace between Great Britain and the United States, in its third article accords to the people of the United States the rights of fishery on the coasts of His Majesty's dominions in America which they had previously enjoyed as British subjects. By way of exception, it is stated that they shall not have the right to dry or cure fish on the island of Newfoundland or in any settled parts of Nova Scotia, the Magdalen Islands, or Newfoundland.

After the war of 1812–1814, numbers of American fishing vessels were seized by British cruisers for following their trade in the waters covered by the above article; and upon protest His Majesty's Government took the ground that the agreement of 1783 had been abrogated by the war. The result, after long negotiation, was the first article in the Convention of Commerce, 1818, which defines anew the rights and privileges of the inhabitants of the United States in the North Atlantic fisheries.

As most of the subsequent controversies, culminating in the great arbitration of 1909, turned on the interpretation of this Article, it must be reproduced here *in extenso:*

Whereas differences have arisen respecting the liberty claimed by the United States, for the Inhabitants thereof, to take, dry, and cure fish, on certain Coasts, Bays, Harbours, and Creeks, of His Britannic Majesty's Dominions, in America; it is agreed between the High Contracting Parties, that the Inhabitants of the said United States shall have, for ever, in common with the Subjects of His Britannic Majesty, the liberty to take fish of every kind, on that part of the southern Coast of Newfoundland, which extends from Cape Ray to the Rameau Islands, on the western and northern Coast of Newfoundland, from the said Cape Ray to the Quirpon Islands, on the shores of the Magdalen Islands, and also on the Coasts, Bays, Harbours and Creeks, from Mount Joly, on the southern Coast of Labrador, to and through the Straits of Belleisle, and thence northwardly indefinitely along the Coast; without prejudice, however, to any of the exclusive rights of the Hudson Bay Company; and that the American fishermen shall also have liberty, for ever, to dry and cure fish in any of the unsettled Bays, Harbours, and Creeks, of the southern part of the Coast of Newfoundland hereabove described, and of the Coast of Labrador; but so soon as the same, or any portion thereof, shall be settled, it shall not be lawful for the said Fishermen to dry or cure fish at such portion so settled, without previous agreement for such purpose, with the Inhabitants, Proprietors or Possessors of the ground. And the United States hereby renounce for ever, any liberty heretofore enjoyed or claimed by the Inhabitants thereof, to take, dry, or cure fish, on or within three marine miles of any of the Coasts, Bays, Creeks, or Harbours, of His Britannic Majesty's Dominions in America, not included within the abovementioned limits; provided, however, that the American Fishermen shall be admitted to enter such Bays, or Harbours, for the purpose of shelter and of repairing damages therein, of purchasing wood, and of obtaining water; and for no other purpose whatever. But they shall be under such restrictions as may be necessary to prevent their taking, drying, or curing fish therein, or in any other manner whatever abusing the privileges hereby reserved to them.[1]

BAY OF FUNDY, 1856

THE earlier disputes centered about the activities of American fishermen in the Bay of Fundy. The colonial view was that the word "bays" in the convention of 1818 meant bodies of water known as bays at that time, and that the three marine miles of reserved water should be measured from a line running from headland to headland. This was the principle adopted in the Nova Scotia Hovering Act of 1836, and under its provisions American vessels were seized in the Bay of Fundy and other bays ten and more miles off shore. In a letter of March 10, 1845, addressed to the American Minister to the Court of St. James's, Lord Aberdeen maintained the same interpretation on behalf of the British Government. By way of amicable concession, however, he agreed that Americans should thenceforward be allowed to fish anywhere in the Bay of Fundy outside three miles from shore and from the entrance of minor bays.[2]

The United States refused to admit the legality of the British interpretation, arguing that the "bays" in which she had in 1818 re-

1. *Treaties and Agreements,* p. 15.
2. *North Atlantic Coast Fisheries Arbitration* (Washington, Government Printing Office, 1912), Vol. IV, Appendix, pp. 240–241.

nounced the right to fish were only the small coastal indentations, and that in general the three miles of territorial water must be measured, not from lines joining headlands, but from the winding line of the coast. Outside the Bay of Fundy, however, His Majesty's Government, after its proposal of further leniency had been vigorously snubbed by the colonies, stood by what it regarded as its legal rights, and the interference of British cruisers with New England vessels brought an American force to the fishing grounds. Matters had come near the breaking point before the Reciprocity Treaty of 1854 brought temporary relaxation.

Two American shipowners' claims arising out of these troubles came before the commission appointed under a convention of 1853. They had to do with the seizure of the *Washington* in 1843 more than ten miles from shore in the Bay of Fundy, and the seizure of the *Argus* off Cow Bay, Cape Breton, in 1844. The *Argus* was taken in the open sea, admittedly more than three miles beyond the headlands, and her owners were awarded $2,000. But the case of the *Washington* brought the legal claim to the Bay of Fundy fairly before the commission, and the finding is therefore of considerable interest. Before examining it, we must look at the composition and powers of the commission and seek the reasons for the outstanding success with which it handled the large number of claims submitted to it.

The convention of 1853 was concluded with a view to the settlement of all outstanding claims, presented since the signature of the Treaty of Ghent on December 24, 1814, on the part of American citizens against the British Government and on the part of British subjects against the Government of the United States. One commissioner was to be appointed by each Government, and these two were to choose an umpire to decide cases on which they differed. If they could not agree on a choice, each was to name one person and from the two so named one was to be selected by lot on each occasion when the commissioners differed in their views on a particular case.

The American Commissioner, Nathaniel Upham, at one time judge of the Supreme Court of New Hampshire, expressed a strong desire to avoid recourse to lot. The disagreement of the commissioners would, he pointed out, be known to the claimants and would impair their confidence in an umpire whom one commissioner did not regard as a suitable person for the office. His reasoning, reënforced by the record of what happened in the slave claims under the convention of 1822,[3] is sufficient to relegate to the limbo of unsound methods this device for the event of disagreement. When commissioners cannot agree on an umpire, the choice is better left to an impartial outsider.

The British Commissioner, Mr. (afterward Sir Edmond) Hornby, met his American colleague more than half way. He inclined at first to the view that the umpire should be a foreigner. Mr. Upham objected to the selection of any member of the diplomatic corps in London, partly because similar claims might be pending between his government and the United States and he might accordingly be prejudiced against the American claimant, and partly for a more general reason which has a good deal to commend it. The diplomatist must as far as possible keep the favor of the government to which he is accredited, and may therefore hesitate to give judgment against it. Hornby finally agreed that, as the commission was to sit in London, the appointment of an American umpire would redress the balance. Eventually the choice fell upon Joshua Bates, a New Englander who, during his long residence in England, had risen to the position of senior member of the financial house of Baring Brothers.

The London Commission dealt with 115 claims, 75 against the United States and 40 against Great Britain. Twelve of the American claims were allowed, 27 dismissed, 1 withdrawn. Fifty-two British claims were dismissed, 19 allowed, and 4 withdrawn. The umpire was called upon to adjudicate in 33 cases. He allowed 10 claims against the United States and the same number against Great Britain. He dismissed 4 of those presented by the United States and 9 of those presented by Great Britain. His complete impartiality was admitted on both sides.

Such was the tribunal before which the case of the *Washington* came. Messrs. Upham and Hornby disagreed, and it went to Mr. Bates as umpire. The umpire awarded $3,000 to the owners. On the British argument for the territoriality of the Bay of Fundy he observed, after pointing out that this arm of the sea was from 65 to 75 miles in width and had several bays on its coast, "thus the word 'bay,' as applied to this great body of water, has the same meaning

3. Moore, *op. cit.*, pp. 350–390.

as that applied to the Bay of Biscay, the Bay of Bengal, over which no nation can have the right to assume sovereignty." In regard to the headland doctrine, he noted that the treaty made no mention of headlands, and that in any case one headland of the Bay of Fundy was situated in the United States. In passing, he cites as a "proper limit" that adopted in the Anglo-French treaty of August 2, 1839, where

it is agreed that the distance of three miles fixed as the general limit for the exclusive right of fishing upon the coasts of the two countries shall, with respect to bays, the mouths of which do not exceed ten miles in width, be measured from a straight line drawn from headland to headland.

We shall find the same criterion recommended by the North Atlantic Fisheries Tribunal in 1909.[4]

RECIPROCITY TREATY OF 1854

RESERVED FISHERIES, 1855–1866

In the Reciprocity Treaty of 1854, the United States got back the liberty to fish in certain British-American coastal waters which had been surrendered in the Convention of Commerce of 1818.[5] At the same time similar privileges were granted to British fishermen along the Atlantic coast of the United States as far south as the thirty-sixth parallel. It was stipulated, however, that these privileges in both cases should extend only to the sea fisheries, and that the salmon and shad fisheries, and all fisheries in rivers and mouths of rivers, should be reserved for the home fishermen.

In order to prevent disputes as to what was meant by "rivers and mouths of rivers," provision was made in the same treaty for a commission to examine the coasts and designate the places reserved from the common right of fishing. The usual mode of appointment was adopted, each of the high contracting parties naming one commissioner, and these two being instructed to choose an umpire by com-

4. *North Atlantic Coast Fisheries Arbitration,* Vol. IV, Appendix, pp. 365–366.
5. See p. 24, above.

mon accord or, if they disagreed, by lot from two persons designated, one by each commissioner.

The two commissioners were duly appointed, and met at Halifax
in August, 1855, to begin their work. They disagreed at once as to
the mouth of the Buctouche River and the Miramichi River in New
Brunswick. The work of examination, with frequent disagreement,
went on until 1866, and was not quite finished when the treaty itself
came to an end by denunciation on the part of the United States. In
that period the personnel of the commission changed several times
by reason of resignation or death.

The early stages of the proceedings, beginning as they did with
immediate disagreement, were marked by a good deal of acerbity.
Mr. Cushman of Maine and Mr. Perley of New Brunswick were the
American and British appointees, respectively. They attempted in
1857, having considerable arrears of conflicting views, to select an
umpire, but were driven to taking lots. The Hon. John Hamilton
Gray of New Brunswick, Mr. Perley's choice, became umpire.

To Mr. Gray were referred the Miramichi and Buctouche and
twenty-four streams in Prince Edward Island. The latter were small
fresh-water streams flowing in some cases into long and wide inlets
of the sea. The British Commissioner had insisted on classifying
them as reserved rivers, while the American Commissioner argued
that they were merely sea creeks and so open to common fishing
under the express terms of the treaty. Mr. Gray, as umpire, decided
in favor of the British case in the Buctouche and Miramichi and in
eighteen of the Prince Edward Island streams. The American Commissioner was not satisfied with the decision, while the American
surveyor assisting in the work described it in a letter to General
Cass, Secretary of State, as flagrantly partial.[6]

Mr. Cushman demanded that a different umpire should be selected
for the settlement of any future disagreements, and invoked a verbal
understanding to this effect arrived at between himself and Mr.
Perley before Mr. Gray's appointment. Mr. Perley, however, now
took the view that the understanding referred to was incompatible
with the treaty. His attention, he said, had in the interval been
drawn to the fact that the treaty, on its true interpretation, re-

6. Moore, *op. cit.,* p. 431.

quired the commissioners to select one umpire only for the solution of all differences between them, empowering them to name another only if the first should have to be replaced owing to his death, incapacity, or refusal to act.

The British Foreign Office, while declining to reopen the awards already made, did not uphold Mr. Perley in the matter of the umpire. In a note to Lord Lyons, British Minister in Washington, Earl Russell writes:

> . . . in cases in which the Commissioners may disagree it is indifferent to Her Majesty's Government who is selected to arbitrate between them, provided he be a gentleman of strict integrity, and with a sufficient acquaintance of the subject to be brought before him.[7]

No new umpire was appointed, however, nor were any further differences submitted to Mr. Gray. Mr. Cushman had resigned in 1858, and with his successors Mr. Perley and his successor, Joseph Howe, were able to complete, in agreement, the process of delimitation on all but a small section of the coast of Newfoundland and of Virginia. The work there would doubtless have been finished if the Reciprocity Treaty had not come to an end in 1866.

The history of the delimitation of these reserved fisheries proves again the justice of the views expressed by Mr. Upham, American member of the London Commission of 1853, on choosing umpires by lot.[8]

The work done under the treaty of 1854 was not entirely wasted, in spite of the termination of that arrangement. For the fisheries agreements were revived in the Treaty of Washington of 1871, and came into operation for a further thirteen years. Article XX of the Treaty of Washington adopts the findings of the commission of 1854.[9] Those findings have also provided definitions used in subsequent statutes. Thus the mouth of the St. Lawrence, a point of great importance in the delimitation of Canadian territorial waters, had been fixed by the Commission of 1854 at a line drawn from Cap Chat on the south shore to Pointe des Monts[10] on the north. The Statute 1 Edward VII, 1901, c. 33, declares that the inland waters of Canada include the River St. Lawrence as far seaward as this line.

7. Moore, *op. cit.,* p. 431.   8. See p. 26, above.
9. *Treaties and Agreements,* p. 44.   10. Moore, *op. cit.,* p. 445.

THE HALIFAX COMMISSION, 1877

THE Treaty of Washington, 1871, granted to American fishermen the liberty to take fish of every kind except shellfish on the sea coasts and in the bays, harbors, and creeks of Quebec, Nova Scotia, New Brunswick, and Prince Edward Island, without restriction to any distance from the shore; and to land upon those coasts to dry nets and cure fish.

Similar liberty on the coasts of the United States as far south as the thirty-ninth parallel was given to British fishermen.

As in the treaty of 1854, the salmon and shad fisheries, and all other fisheries in rivers and the mouths of rivers, were reserved for British and American fishermen, respectively; and the places designated by the commissioners working under the treaty of 1854 were accepted as reserved within the meaning of this clause.

Provision was made for the designation, by a commission similar to that set up in 1854, of any further places claimed by either Government as reserved under the treaty, but apparently no occasion arose for recourse to proceedings of this nature.

On the British side it was maintained during the negotiations that the privileges granted to American fishermen on the Canadian coasts were a great deal more valuable than those granted to British fishermen on the coasts of the United States. The American Government refused to admit this, but agreed in the resulting treaty that commissioners should be appointed to consider this matter and to determine what compensation, if any, should be paid by the United States to Great Britain.

Article XXIII of the treaty laid down the mode of appointment of the commissioners. One each was to be named by Great Britain and the United States and the third by the two Governments conjointly. If the third commissioner should not be so named within three months after the date when this article came into effect, then he was to be appointed by the representative at London of the Emperor of Austria.

The fisheries articles came into effect on July 1, 1873, but three months of negotiation failed to result in the conjoint choice of a third commissioner. The British Minister at Washington had suggested M. Delfosse, Minister of Belgium to the United States, but

Mr. Fish, the American Secretary of State, objected on the ground that

there were reasons in the political relations between his (M. Delfosse's) government and that of Great Britain why the representative of the former could not be regarded as an independent and indifferent arbitrator. . . .

The Canadian Government, consulted because of its obvious interest, objected to the nomination of any of the diplomats resident at Washington, stating that it would prefer to see the Austrian Minister to the Court of St. James's make the appointment.

Further delay occurred owing to the fact that a new reciprocity treaty, which would have abrogated the provisions of 1871 for a commission to meet at Halifax, was under discussion. It was only in 1875, after the Senate had voted against the new project, that negotiations for the appointment of a third commissioner were resumed. These dragged on until 1877, when Mr. Fish informed the British Government that the United States would not object to the appointment of M. Delfosse if Great Britain suggested his nomination to the Austrian ambassador in London. So it finally came about that M. Delfosse assumed the office, being warmly congratulated on the occasion by Mr. Fish who, in 1873, would have none of him. The details of this negotiation are important in view of the attitude adopted by Congress, the American press, and, finally, the Government itself, on publication of the commission's award.[11]

After meetings stretching from June to November, 1877, during which many witnesses were examined and numerous counsel heard, the commission issued a majority award signed by M. Delfosse and by Sir Alexander Galt, the British Commissioner. This award gave to Great Britain, as compensation for the difference in the privileges granted in the treaty of 1871 to American and British fishermen, respectively, the sum of five and a half million dollars.

Mr. Kellogg, American Commissioner, stated in his dissenting opinion that he found the advantages accruing to Great Britain greater than those accruing to the United States. He also questioned the competence of the commission to make an award otherwise than by unanimous vote.

11. Moore, *op. cit.*, pp. 725–727.

Congress appropriated the necessary sum, but attached to its vote the rider that the President should, before paying, correspond with the British Government on the conformity of the award with the treaty of 1871. There ensued an exchange of letters in which Mr. Evarts, Secretary of State, urged a revision on the ground that the amount was far in excess of the worth of the privileges to the American fishing industry and that any award should have been unanimous. The latter objection he supported by pointing out that the treaty of 1871 set up four boards of arbitration and expressly provided in regard to three of them that a majority decision should be valid. *A contrario,* unanimity must be inferred as a requirement of this fourth commission, which had not been expressly given power to decide by a majority. Mr. Evarts also regretted that the reasoning by which the majority had reached its conclusions had not been set out in the award or in any record. The same was true of Mr. Kellogg's dissenting opinion.

On the question of unanimity, Lord Salisbury in his reply had no difficulty in showing that the general view of the authorities on international law accepted the award of a majority of arbitrators as binding, unless the contrary were expressly stipulated. That is precisely the purpose of establishing arbitral commissions with an uneven number of members. The United States had, moreover, adopted this view in connection with the St. Croix River arbitration in 1796.[12] As for the justice and amount of the compensation, any discussion of that would amount to the reopening of a decision which was essentially final and without appeal.

In 1878 the Government of the United States paid the five and a half million dollars. In doing so, it protested that its action must not be taken as an admission of any obligation, for it persisted in the opinion that the finding was unjust and invalid.

This was submission with bad grace, but in one point at least the American Government was justified in its discontent. The omission of all *rationes decidendi* was a serious defect in the commission's findings. An arbitral tribunal ought to be able to justify both the direction and the amount of its award, and a leaf from the book of the commission which dealt with the Hudson Bay claims in 1869 would have been useful at Halifax. The Halifax award was bound

12. Moore, *op. cit.,* p. 751, note.

to excite unnecessary irritation by its abrupt and arbitrary tone. There is some solace, even to the loser, in sweet reason. Certainly the size of the compensation comes as a shock to the reader perusing the available records and if, as is to be presumed, the commission had good grounds for the amount awarded, they should have stated them. The fact that between them Canada and Newfoundland were claiming $14,880,000 is barely relevant.

THE NORTH-ATLANTIC FISHERIES ARBITRATION, 1910

THE Treaty of Washington, 1871, which renewed the mutual rights of fishing and freedom from customs duties on fish and fish oil granted in 1854, by no means brought about that pacification in the Atlantic fishing industry which it had been designed to achieve. Frequent trouble arose from American violations of regulations enacted by the legislatures in Canada and Newfoundland. Dissatisfaction in the United States led to the termination, in 1885, of the fisheries articles in the Treaty of Washington, and the parties were thrown back on the convention of 1818 for the definition of their rights.

From 1886 on, annual seizures of American vessels for fishing within the three-mile limit, for purchasing bait in ports which the convention of 1818 allowed them to enter only for shelter, repair, or provision of wood and water, for failure to report at customs, for refusal to pay light dues, and for various other infractions of the convention or of local regulations, ran into the hundreds; and diplomatic correspondence between Washington and London was full of emphatic protests on the one side and reassertions of right on the other.

In 1888 a *modus vivendi* was negotiated between Canada and the United States, whereby, on payment of an annual fee, American fishing craft were permitted to enter Canadian ports for the purchase of bait and supplies and for transshipping. With temporary suspensions, this arrangement has been continued up to the present, and it has removed the worst of the American grievances. With Newfoundland, however, the struggle still went on. Laws were there maintained or newly enacted prohibiting (1) the sale of bait, lines, and provisions to foreign fishermen; (2) the employment of New-foundland fishermen by foreign skippers attempting to evade the first prohibition; (3) Sunday fishing; and (4) the use of purse seines. It was the constant protests of the United States against these restrictions in what they regarded as a free-treaty fishery that at last brought about, in 1909, the submission of the whole question of American rights in the coastal fisheries of Newfoundland and Canada to arbitration.

In 1908 there came into effect the first general arbitration treaty between Great Britain and the United States. Article I reads as follows:

Differences which may arise of a legal nature or relating to the inter-pretation of treaties existing between the two Contracting Parties and which it may not have been possible to settle by diplomacy, shall be referred to the Permanent Court of Arbitration established at The Hague by the Convention of the 29th July, 1899, provided, neverthe-less, that they do not affect the vital interests, the independence, or the honour of the two Contracting States, and do not concern the interests of third parties.[13]

This treaty laid it down in the second article that the parties should, before referring any case to the Permanent Court, conclude a special agreement to define clearly, *inter alia*, the matter in dispute and the powers of the arbitrators. Within eight months an elaborate agreement had been drawn up for the submission of the whole dis-pute about the Atlantic fisheries.

By the terms of this agreement (Article 5), the Tribunal was to be chosen from the general list of the members of the Permanent Court, in accordance with Article 45 of the Hague Convention of 1907 on the Settlement of International Disputes. Article 45 of the Hague Convention leaves the composition of the tribunal in the first instance to the choice of the parties, limiting their choice, however, to the members of the Court, a very numerous panel including emi-nent jurists of all the forty-odd adhering states. The Article goes on to provide complete machinery for making the selection in the event of disagreement at any stage of this first process on the part of the litigants. It was unnecessary to have recourse to such machinery,

13. *Treaties and Agreements,* pp. 297–298.

since the two Governments were able to agree upon personnel. The American member was George Gray, judge of the United States Circuit Court of Appeal; the British member was Sir Charles Fitzpatrick, Chief Justice of Canada. Dr. Lammash, professor of international law at Vienna, was chosen as president, while the two other foreign members were the Jonkheer Lohman, Dutch Minister of State, and Señor Drago of the Argentine Republic.

The tribunal so composed held its first assembly at The Hague on June 1, 1910, and heard oral arguments until August 12. Judgment was rendered on September 7, 1910—a very rapid disposal of the case, considering its complexity. The questions put to the tribunal were set out in Article I of the *compromis*. They, and the judgment on each, are summarized in what follows.[14]

Question I. Is the liberty to take fish, accorded forever to the inhabitants of the United States in Article I of the convention of 1818, subject, without the consent of the United States, to reasonable regulation by Great Britain, Canada, or Newfoundland, in respect of (1) the hours, days, or seasons when fish may be taken; (2) the method, means, and implements to be used; (3) any other matters of a similar character?

Answer. The right of Great Britain to make regulations without the consent of the United States, in the form of municipal laws, ordinances, or rules of Great Britain, Canada, or Newfoundland, is inherent in the sovereignty of Great Britain.

The exercise of this right is, however, limited by the convention of 1818 in that such regulations must be made *bona fide* and must not violate the convention.

Regulations which are (1) appropriate or necessary for the protection and preservation of the fisheries, or (2) desirable or necessary on grounds of public order and morals without unnecessarily interfering with the fishery itself, and in both cases equitable and fair as between local and American fishermen, are not inconsistent with the obligation to execute the treaty in good faith, and are therefore reasonable and not in violation of the treaty.

The reasonableness of any regulation, if contested, must be decided by an impartial authority in accordance with the above principles. Here the tribunal, acting under Article IV of the *compromis*

14. *Treaties and Agreements,* pp. 325–342.

which called upon it to recommend rules and procedure for the settlement of future questions regarding the exercise of the liberty of fishing, recommended that this impartial authority should be a Permanent Mixed Fishery Commission for Canada and another for Newfoundland. Each of these was to consist of an expert national appointed by each party with an umpire not a national of either. The mode of selection of the umpire was defined in the recommendations.[15]

Question II. Have the inhabitants of the United States, while exercising the liberties conferred by the convention, a right to employ as members of their fishing crews persons not inhabitants of the United States?

Answer. Yes, because the liberty to take fish is an economic right, the exercise of which includes the right to employ servants, and the treaty does not limit such servants to persons of a distinct nationality or inhabitancy. But non-inhabitants employed as members of the fishing crews derive no benefit or immunity from the treaty; nor does the treaty affect the sovereign right of Great Britain as to aliens, non-inhabitants of the United States, nor the right of Great Britain to regulate the engagement of British subjects, while these aliens or British subjects are on British territory.

This is the most ambiguous part of the whole award. Unless it means only that aliens who are not inhabitants of the United States may fish, not in their own right (which is self-evident and needed no statement), but solely in right of their employers, it appears to contain a contradiction. If they may fish at all in these waters, they do so only in virtue of the treaty. How then can it be said that they derive no "benefit or immunity" from the treaty? "No direct benefit or immunity" would be accurate.

Question III. Can the exercise of the liberties be subjected, without the consent of the United States, to the requirement of entry or report at customhouses or the payment of light or harbor or other dues, or to any other similar requirement, condition, or exaction?

Answer. The requirement that an American fishing vessel should report, if proper conveniences for doing so are at hand, is not unreasonable. There should be no such requirement, however, unless there be reasonably convenient opportunity afforded to report in

15. *Ibid.,* p. 334.

person or by telegraph, either at a customhouse or to a customs official.

But the exercise of the fishing liberty by the inhabitants of the United States should not be subjected to the purely commercial formalities of report, entry, and clearance at a customhouse, nor to light, harbor, or other dues not imposed upon Newfoundland fishermen.

The exercise of the fishing liberty is distinct from the exercise of commercial or trading privileges and it is not competent for Great Britain or her colonies to impose upon the former exactions only appropriate to the latter.

Question IV. Where American fishermen are under the convention permitted to enter certain bays and harbors only for shelter, repairs, wood, or water, may they be required in so entering to pay light, harbor, or other dues, or enter or report at customhouses?

Answer. This privilege is merely one of hospitality and humanity, and its exercise may not be made conditional upon such requirements. But if fishermen so entering remain more than forty-eight hours, they may be required to report, either in person or by telegraph at a customhouse or to a customs official, if reasonably convenient opportunity therefor is afforded.

Question V. From where must be measured the "three marine miles of any of the coasts, bays, creeks or harbours" referred to in Article I of the convention?

Answer. The Tribunal here rejected the claim of the United States that her renunciation of 1818 applied only to bays six miles or less in width and to territorial water, holding that the words of the treaty must apply to every bay on the coast in question which might be reasonably supposed to have been considered as a bay by the negotiators of the treaty. It therefore decided that in the case of bays the three marine miles were to be measured from a straight line drawn across the body of water at the place where it ceased to have the configuration of a bay. At all other places they were to be measured following the sinuosities of the coast.

In order to make this vague "configuration-criterion" applicable in practice, the tribunal went on to recommend that, except in certain bays which it specified, the limits of expulsion should be drawn three miles seaward from a straight line across the bay in the part nearest the entrance at the first point where the width did not exceed ten miles. This ten-mile standard was adopted from certain British agreements with France and Germany and from British instructions to naval officers stationed on North American coasts.

Question VI. Have the inhabitants of the United States the liberty to take fish in the bays, harbors, and creeks on the southern coast of Newfoundland between Cape Ray and Rameau Islands, or on the western and northern coasts of Newfoundland from Cape Ray to Quirpon Islands, or on the Magdalen Islands?

This question arose from the fact that the treaty did not specify in the case of Newfoundland and the Magdalen Islands, as it did in regard to the southern coast of Labrador, "bays, harbours and creeks"; but mentioned only the "coasts" of Newfoundland and the "shore" of the Magdalen Islands.

Answer. The words "part of the southern coast . . . from . . . to . . ." and "western and northern coasts . . . from . . . to . . ." clearly indicated one uninterrupted coastline; and there is no reason to read into the word "coasts" a contradistinction to bays, in order to exclude bays. On the contrary, the words "liberty, forever, to dry and cure fish in any of the unsettled bays, harbours and creeks of the southern part of the coast of Newfoundland hereabove described" indicate that in the meaning of the convention, as in all the preceding treaties relating to the same territories, the words "coast," "coasts," "harbours," "bays," etc., are used without attaching to the word "coast" the specific meaning of excluding bays.

The convention expressly allows the liberty to dry and cure in the unsettled bays, etc., of the southern part of the coast of Newfoundland, and this shows that *a fortiori* the taking of fish in those bays is also allowed.

The same reasoning applies to the "shores of the Magdalen Islands," and the answer to the whole of Question VI is therefore in the affirmative.

Question VII. Are the inhabitants of the United States whose vessels resort to the treaty coast for the purpose of exercising the liberties of the convention entitled to have for those vessels, when duly authorized by the United States in that behalf, the commercial privileges on the treaty coasts accorded by agreement or otherwise to United States trading vessels generally?

Answer. There is nothing in the convention to disentitle such vessels to commercial privileges accorded by agreement or otherwise to United States vessels generally. But they cannot at the same time and during the same voyage exercise their treaty rights and enjoy their commercial privileges, because treaty rights and commercial privileges are submitted to different rules, regulations, and restraints.

There was only one dissent from any finding of the tribunal. Dr. Drago disagreed with the remaining arbiters on the answer to Question V. In his opinion the convention was intended to exclude American fishermen (except when they were explicitly admitted) only from such bays as were British territorial water. Accordingly he held that the tribunal was called upon for a definition of what were British bays on the treaty coasts. For the purpose of such a decision, he would have adopted as part of the award, and not simply as a recommendation, the ten-mile measure consistently used in British fisheries agreements.[16]

The almost universal unanimity in this important decision, disposing of a series of conflicts that reached back over a century, is a notable tribute to the personnel of the tribunal and to the provisions of the Hague conventions for the pacific settlement of international disputes. It doubtless goes some way to account for the fact that neither Great Britain nor the United States took advantage of the right expressly reserved in Article 10 of the *compromis* to demand a revision of the award within five days of its promulgation.

In 1912 an agreement was concluded between Great Britain and the United States to give effect to the tribunal's recommendations on the subject of reasonableness of regulations, and on the definition of reserved bays. Provision was therein made for the mixed fisheries commissions proposed by the arbiters, for notification of new laws to the United States, the period within which protest could be lodged, and the convocation of the commissions; and broad lines of procedure were laid down for the guidance of commissioners. The agreement went on to specify the limit of a number of named bays "contiguous to the territory of the Dominion of Canada"; and for others similarly contiguous, but not specified, adopted the tribunal's

16. *Treaties and Agreements,* pp. 342–348.

ten-mile measure. The text states that the parties do not understand the award as covering Hudson Bay, and, further, that the delimitation of Newfoundland bays did not for the present need consideration.[17]

FUR-SEAL ARBITRATION, 1893

I HAVE sacrificed chronology to matter, preferring to deal with the
Atlantic fisheries disputes in a continuous narrative. We must now
turn back seventeen years and transfer ourselves from the northeast
to the northwest coast of the continent. The Behring Sea fur-seal
arbitration is one of the *causes célèbres* of Canadian-American history by reason not only of the issues involved, the tensity of feeling
with which it was attended, and the impressive staging of the pro-
ceeding, but also of the important results achieved.

In 1867 Russia ceded to the United States for the sum of $7,200,-
000 all her territory and dominion on the continent of America and
the adjacent islands. On the east the limit of the cession was the
boundary between the Russian and British territories so imperfectly
defined in the Anglo-Russian convention of 1825, on the west a line
running due north from a point in the middle of the Behring Strait
and southwest from the same point, passing to the west of St. Lawrence Island and the Aleutian Archipelago.

Between 1868 and 1873, Congress enacted a series of statutes
extending to the area thus ceded the laws of the United States on
customs, commerce, and navigation. Among other things they prohibited any person from killing fur seals within the territory and
its waters except under lease or permit from the Secretary of the
Treasury. No firearms were to be used nor any other means employed in the industry tending to drive the seals from their habitual
breeding grounds. In 1870 the Secretary of the Treasury leased to
the Alaska Commercial Company for twenty years the privilege of
killing 100,000 seals annually on the islands of St. Paul and St.
George, known together as the Pribilof Group.

Conflict between the exclusive claims of the United States and the
activities of British Columbian sealers came to a head in 1886, with
the seizure by the American revenue cutter *Corwin* of three Cana-

17. *Ibid.,* pp. 456–459.

dian schooners in Behring Sea more than fifty miles from land. On a charge of killing seals in violation of Section 1956 of the Revised Statutes of the United States, Judge Dawson of the United States district court at Sitka condemned these vessels to be sold, and sentenced their officers to fines and imprisonment.

After a year of sharp protests from the British Government, the President of the United States ordered the release of ships and officers. This order had not been executed on October 12, 1887, and in the meantime six more schooners had been seized and condemned by the same judge.

In this same year Mr. Bayard, American Secretary of State, opened negotiations with Great Britain, France, Russia, and Japan for an arrangement to protect the Behring seal fisheries. He proposed that there be a closed season between April 15 and November 1 during which no seals should be killed by firearms or other destructive weapons. Lord Salisbury, British Foreign Secretary, was disposed to agree, reserving the question of due compensation for the seizures already made and with the understanding that they should not be repeated pending the conclusion of a general agreement. Representation from the Canadian Government caused him to halt.

Feeling on the Canadian Pacific coast had been running high over what was regarded as an arrogant assumption of sovereignty in the open sea on the part of the United States, and a totally unwarranted interference with an industry from which considerable numbers of Canadians gained their living. The government at Ottawa prevailed upon the Foreign Office not to commit itself until it had received a memorandum setting out the Canadian view of the whole matter.

Upon this intervention from Ottawa, Mr. Phelps, American Minister to the Court of St. James's, made the following comment in a report to Washington:

It is proposed by the colony of a foreign nation, in defiance of the joint remonstrance of all the countries interested, to destroy this business by the indiscriminate slaughter and extermination of the animals in question, in the open neighbouring sea, during the period of gestation, when the common dictates of humanity ought to protect them, were there no interest at all involved. And it is suggested that we are prevented from defending ourselves against such depredations because the sea at a certain distance from the coast is free. The same line of argument would take under its protection piracy and the slave trade, when prosecuted in the open sea. . . .[18]

The aspersion upon the "colony" is a sharp one, hardly justified by the circumstances. The Canadian authorities were in possession of sufficient data, mostly from official American sources, to make it very doubtful at that time whether the sweeping restrictions proposed by Mr. Bayard were necessary. The memorandum, for which Lord Salisbury had been requested to wait, came to hand in August, 1888. It was drawn up by George (afterward Sir George) E. Foster, acting Minister of Marine and Fisheries, and it brings out two well-substantiated objections to the American proposals. In the first place, Mr. Foster was able to show, by the collation of American reports, that the average annual slaughter of seals was only a small fraction of their natural increase. Secondly, he emphasized the fact, which even the uninitiated Foreign Office must have suspected, that Mr. Bayard's plan would exclude all but American sealers from any effective participation in the catch. The memorandum reads:

It is a well-known fact that seals do not begin to enter the Behring's Sea until the middle or end of May; they have practically all left those waters by the end of October. The establishment of the proposed close season, therefore, prohibits the taking of seals during the whole year. . . .

But the United States Government propose to allow seals to be killed by their own citizens on the rookeries, the only places where they haul out in Alaska, during June, July, September and October. . . .

It is to be noted that the area proposed by Mr. Bayard to be affected by the close season virtually covers the whole portion of the Behring's Sea in which the exclusive right of sealing has, during 1886 and 1887, been practically maintained by the United States Government. To this is added a part of the North Pacific Ocean, north of 50° of north latitude, and which commands the approach of the seals to the passes leading into Behring's Sea. By the adoption of this area and close season the United States would gain, by consent, what she has for two years held in defiance of international law and the protests of Great Britain and Canada.

The device, if successful, would feed and perpetuate the rookeries on

18. *Fur Seal Arbitration: Appendix to the Case of the United States* (Washington, Government Printing Office, 1892), I, 181–183.

St. Paul and St. George Islands, and add immensely to their value, while it cuts off at one blow the most valuable portion of the high seas from all participation by the sealers of all other nations.[19]

The result of this memorandum was a suspension of negotiations. Furthur seizure of Canadian vessels took place in 1889. Negotiations were resumed with proposals from both sides for a *modus vivendi* and arbitration of the legal questions involved, including the legality or illegality of the seizures and condemnations, and the right of the United States to exercise the general control which she claimed over the seal fishery. It was not until June 15, 1891, however, that the two Governments agreed, pending arbitration, to stop the killing of seals by their subjects in the Behring Sea and on its islands until the following May.

This was followed by an agreement, dated December 18, 1891, under which each Government appointed two commissioners to investigate all facts bearing on seal life in the Behring Sea and to suggest measures for its preservation. The British commissioners were Sir George Baden-Powell, M.P., and Professor George M. Dawson, of the Canadian Geological Survey.[20]

In spite of bitter protests from the commercial interests on both sides against the stoppage in their operations, the two Governments proceeded with their efforts to reach a settlement of the many questions which by this time had gathered about the Behring seals. On February 29, 1892, they signed a treaty of arbitration, and in the following April they renewed the *modus vivendi* suspending sealing until the arbitral tribunal should have rendered its decision.

This body was to be composed of seven arbitrators, two appointed by each party, one appointed by the President of France, one by the King of Italy, and one by the King of Sweden and Norway. It was

19. *Fur Seal Arbitration* (Washington, Government Printing Office, 1895), V, 237–239. See also p. 599 for Sir Julian Pauncefote's considered view on the whole question. He concludes that "the enquiry had failed to establish the contention of the United States Government that the absolute prohibition of pelagic sealing is necessary for the preservation of the fur-seal species."

20. These arrangements were concurred in by the Canadian Government which was, indeed, largely responsible for their content. See, e.g., the volume cited in preceding note, pp. 463, 599, 767.

agreed that they should be jurists of distinguished reputation in their respective countries.

Great Britain named Lord Hannen, of the English Court of Appeal, and Sir John Thompson, Minister of Justice for Canada; the United States, Mr. Justice Harlan, Justice of the Supreme Court, and United States Senator John Morgan. The other members of the tribunal were Baron de Courcil, Marquis Visconti Venosta, and Mr. Gregors Gram. Paris was specified in the treaty as the place where the sittings were to be held; they began on February 23, 1893, and came to an end with the rendering of the award on August 15 of the same year.

Five questions were formulated in Article VI of the treaty of 1892 for decision by this tribunal. They are given seriatim below, each followed by the relevant portion of the award.

Question I. What exclusive jurisdiction in Behring Sea, and what exclusive rights in the seal fisheries therein, did Russia assert and exercise before the cession of Alaska to the United States?

Answer (Senator Morgan dissenting). In 1821 Russia claimed jurisdiction in the Behring Sea for 100 Italian miles from shore. In negotiating the treaties of 1824 with the United States and 1825 with Great Britain, however, she agreed that her jurisdiction should be restricted to cannon shot from shore; and from that time until the cession she never asserted or exercised any exclusive jurisdiction in Behring Sea; or any exclusive rights in the seal fisheries therein beyond the ordinary limit of territorial waters.

Question II. How far were these claims as to the seal fisheries recognized and conceded by Great Britain?

Answer (Senator Morgan dissenting). Since no claim was made, there could be no question of recognition, but the tribunal made assurance doubly sure by replying here, in effect, "Not at all."

Question III. Was the body of water now known as Behring Sea included in the phrase "Pacific Ocean" as used in the treaty of 1825 between Great Britain and Russia; and what rights, if any, in Behring Sea, were held and exclusively exercised by Russia after the said treaty?

Answer. Article I of the treaty of 1825 ran in part as follows:

It is agreed that the respective subjects of the high contracting

Parties shall not be troubled or molested, in any part of the Great Ocean, commonly called the Pacific Ocean, either in navigating the same, in fishing therein, etc.[21]

It was contended on behalf of the United States that "Great Ocean" and "Pacific Ocean" as here used did not include Behring Sea, and accordingly that Russia had not by this article surrendered her claim to special rights in that sea.

The arbitrators unanimously decided that the phrase "Pacific Ocean" included Behring Sea.

As to the second part of the question, the tribunal (Senator Morgan dissenting) merely repeated the substance of its answer to Question I.

Question IV. Did not all the rights of Russia as to jurisdiction and as to the seal fisheries in Behring Sea, east of the water boundary, in the treaty between the United States and Russia of March 30, 1867, pass unimpaired to the United States under that treaty?

Answer (unanimous). Yes.

Question V. Has the United States any right, and if so, what right, of protection or property in the fur seals frequenting the islands of the United States in Behring Sea when such seals are found outside the ordinary three-mile limit?

Answer (Mr. Justice Harlan and Senator Morgan dissenting). The United States has no right of protection or profit in these seals when found outside the said limit.

The treaty of arbitration had provided in its seventh article that

if the determination of the foregoing questions . . . shall leave the subject in such position that the concurrence of Great Britain is necessary to the establishment of regulations for the proper protection and preservation of the fur-seal in, or habitually resorting to, the Behring's Sea, the Arbitrators shall then determine what concurrent regulations outside the jurisdictional limits of the respective Governments are necessary, and over what water such regulations should extend, and to aid them in that determination, the Report of a Joint Commission, to be appointed by the respective Governments, shall be laid before them, with such other evidence as either Government may submit.

21. *Fur Seal Arbitration,* IV, 42.

This article constituted the tribunal a sort of joint legislature for the two parties within the defined limits, an unusual and interesting procedure. Its result was a series of drastic restrictions on the sealing industry, enacted as a whole by a majority of four to three, Mr. Justice Harlan, Sir John Thompson, and Senator Morgan dissenting. These regulations may be summarized as follows: (1) both Governments to prohibit sealing at all times within a zone of sixty miles around the Pribilof Islands; (2) a close season outside this zone from May 1 to July 31; (3) only sailing vessels to be used in seal hunting; (4) no nets, firearms, or explosives to be used.

In an added declaration the arbitrators pointed out that these regulations were, as required by the treaty of arbitration, applicable in the high seas only, and recommended that further regulations should be agreed on by the parties for application within the sovereignty of each. Two members of the tribunal, Baron de Courcil and Mr. Justice Harlan, approved a recommendation that both Governments should prohibit all killing of fur seals, either on land or sea, for a period of at least one year.

Both the United States and Great Britain passed acts in 1894 to give effect to the regulations determined by the arbiters. No agreement was arrived at, however, for the suspension suggested by Baron de Courcil and Mr. Justice Harlan.

There remained the matter of compensation due for the seizure of Canadian vessels engaged in the industry. In Article VIII of the treaty, the parties had declared themselves unable to agree upon a reference which would include this question, but had provided that either might submit to the arbitrators any question of fact involved in such claims and ask for a finding, the question of liability upon the facts found to be the subject of further negotiation. Great Britain had accordingly submitted the Canadian claims, and the arbitrators had unanimously and in agreement with the agent and counsel for the United States, found the facts as stated in the case of twenty ships and thirteen of their officers.

In subsequent negotiations Great Britain agreed to accept $425,-000 in full and final settlement; but Congress failed to appropriate this money, and a convention was concluded on February 8, 1896, setting up a commission to investigate and determine all claims for the seizure of shipping, imprisonment of officers, and any other injuries inflicted by United States officials. In December, 1897, this commission awarded to Great Britain the sum of $473,151.26.

The composition and proceedings of the commission which finally settled the long-standing grievance of Canada over the seizures of 1886–1890 are worthy of notice. The two commissioners were to be "persons learned in the law," and in fact two judges were appointed, one the Hon. George King of the Supreme Court of Canada, the other the Hon. William Putnam of the United States Circuit Court. It had been arranged in the Convention of 1896 that if they failed to agree over any given claim the two Governments, or in the event of their disagreement the President of the Swiss Confederation, should appoint an umpire. The decisions, as it transpired, were all agreed, and no umpire had to be appointed—another of the many instances of successful recourse to persons of high judicial office for the settlement of Canadian-American disputes.[22]

The long process of arbitration, regulation, and adjudication which has just been described did not put an end to international difficulties in Behring Sea. From the United States came more or less constant pressure for the complete abolition of pelagic sealing on the ground that, if it was allowed to continue, the complete extermination of the herds was only a matter of limited time. For many years Canada refused to forbid her citizens sealing outside the limits defined by the Paris tribunal. The matter was one of those referred to the Joint High Commission which assembled at Quebec in 1898; but, as every one knows, that effort broke up on the reefs of the Alaskan boundary.

It was not until 1911 that Great Britain and the United States reached an agreement to prohibit all pelagic sealing in the Pacific Ocean north of 35° north latitude and east of the 180th meridian. This left the United States, by virtue of her ownership of the Pribilof Islands, alone in a position to pursue the industry, and Article 2 of the treaty assigned to Canada one fifth of the annual catch. Scarcely, however, had this treaty been concluded when it was superseded by the convention of the same year between Great Britain, the United States, Japan, and Russia, which put an end to pelagic sealing in the whole Pacific from the thirtieth parallel northward. To Canada was assigned: 15 per cent of the American catch on the

22. *Treaties and Agreements,* pp. 98–104.

Pribilof Islands; 15 per cent of the Russian catch on the Commander Islands; 10 per cent of the Japanese catch on the Robben Islands.

The convention was concluded for a period of fifteen years, being terminable by twelve months' notice given at any time from the end of the fourteenth year onward.

CHAPTER IV

INLAND WATERWAYS

THE boundary between the United States and Canada runs for many hundreds of miles along rivers and lakes, while the remainder of its course is intersected by numerous rivers. Diversion, obstruction, or pollution of these waters on one side of the line must in the nature of things affect interests on the other, and conflicts were bound to occur over measures to promote navigation, irrigation, sanitation, and the development of power. A long series of treaties had secured to the nationals of both countries the common right of navigation in boundary waters and connecting canals, in the St. Lawrence where it passes through Canadian territory to the sea, and in the Columbia. It was not until 1894–1895, however, that any action began to be taken toward the establishment of permanent organs of regulation and control. At the irrigation congresses held in those years at Denver and Albuquerque, respectively, plans were discussed by American, Canadian, and Mexican delegates, and a resolution adopted urging the United States to set up an international commission to act with the Mexican and Canadian authorities to settle conflicting claims relating to the international streams of the continent.

The Canadian Government followed up this beginning in 1896 by signifying through the British Ambassador at Washington its wish to participate in some plan of joint regulation. In these overtures the name of Mexico disappears, and the subsequent steps concern only Canada and her neighbor. In 1902 the President was requested by act of Congress to invite Great Britain to join in the formation of an international commission of three members from the United States and three from Canada whose duty it should be to investigate and report upon the "conditions and uses of the waters adjacent to the boundary." The invitation was dispatched in July, 1902, and the American commissioners appointed in the same year; but it was not until 1905 that Canada appointed her representatives and the commission was set up.

The International Waterways Commission of 1905 submitted to

the Governments a series of reports terminating in 1911. These had to do with diversions at Niagara, Sault Ste Marie, and Chicago, and with the location of the boundary line through Lake Erie. The commission, however, had only commenced its work when it began to feel the need of larger powers. It was purely a body of reference, called upon to make reports; what was needed was a treaty to determine, and a permanent commission empowered to enforce, the principles which should govern the entire use of lakes and streams forming or intersecting the line of division between the two countries. The two Governments were repeatedly recommended to conclude such a treaty and establish such a commission. Negotiations to this end were begun in 1907, bearing fruit in the Boundary Waters Treaty signed at Washington on January 11, 1909, and ratified on May 5 of the same year.[1]

This treaty defines what are boundary waters; confirms the common right of navigation therein and in Lake Michigan; limits to specific dimensions the diversion of water for power purposes from the Niagara River; provides that the St. Mary and Milk rivers in Montana, Alberta, and Saskatchewan shall be treated as one stream for the purposes of irrigation and power, and stipulates that the measurement and apportionment of their water shall be carried out under the supervision of an international joint commission; prohibits pollution; makes any use, obstruction, or diversion of boundary waters other than those already permitted conditional upon the approval of an international joint commission; and, finally, lays down the constitution and powers of such a commission.

The International Joint Commission consists of six members, three appointed by the President of the United States and three by His Majesty upon recommendation of the Governor in Council of the Dominion of Canada. It has three types of functions: (a) compulsory jurisdiction in questions of diversion, obstruction, or new uses affecting the natural level or flow; (b) the duty to investigate and report, at the request of either Government, upon any question or difference involving the rights, obligations, or interests of either

1. For a brief history and bibliography, see C. J. Chacko, *The International Joint Commission between the United States of America and the Dominion of Canada* (New York, 1932), pp. 71–78, or *Papers Relating to the Work of the International Joint Commission* (Ottawa, 1929), pp. 103–104.

party along the common frontier; (c) to serve as an arbitral tribunal upon consent of both parties for the decision of any difference between them.

The first two functions have been repeatedly exercised, to the great benefit of common interests; but the commission has never yet been called upon to act as an arbitral tribunal. It has hitherto been manned with a view to the adjustment of claims requiring long and generally technical investigation, and has handled the many important matters referred to it with most remarkable impartiality and unanimity. There have been fifteen applications for permission to divert or obstruct water, and six references for investigation and report. In every case, excepting the Rainy River Improvement Company's application (1913) which was dismissed for lack of jurisdiction by a majority of four to two,[2] and excepting a reservation filed by the American members in the final report on the Lake of the Woods,[3] its decisions have been reached without a dissenting voice. The question remains, in spite of this notable record, whether the body is equally well calculated to deal competently with disputes which have reached the point of requiring arbitration in the strict sense of the term. The history of arbitration between the two countries tends to show that the best success in matters of urgent import and charged with national feeling is to be obtained by recourse to personnel of high judicial position or of such eminence in the legal world as to have gained inclusion in the panel of the Permanent Court of Arbitration.

Among the factors contributing to the establishment of permanent machinery for the regulation of boundary waters were three long-standing conflicts of riparian claims. These had to do, first, with the use of the St. Mary and Milk rivers in Alberta and Montana for irrigation; second, with the levels of the Lake of the Woods; and, third, with power development in the St. Mary's River from

2. R. A. MacKay, "The International Joint Commission between the United States and Canada," *American Journal of International Law* (1928), Vol. 22, pp. 292–318, reprinted in *Papers Relating to the Work of the I.J.C.*, pp. 71–100. See latter publication, p. 86.

3. *Ibid.*, p. 89. And see the *Final Report of the International Joint Commission on the Lake of the Woods Reference* (Washington, Government Printing Office, 1917), pp. 73, 76–79.

Lake Superior into Lake Huron. For the first the treaty itself made direct provision; the others were among the many problems which have been submitted in their entirety to the International Joint Commission. But the first also was destined to furnish occasion for long hearings, some of them on the spot, by the commission; for though the treaty decided that the St. Mary and Milk rivers were to be treated as one stream for purposes of irrigation and power, and referred the measurement and apportionment of their waters to the joint agency of the United States reclamation officers and the Canadian irrigation officers, it yet required that the commission should supervise this work. The reclamation and irrigation officers were unable to agree, and in 1915 individuals, corporations, and the national departments concerned began appearing before the commission to present their grievances and argue their claims. A difference of opinion as to what tributaries had been intended for division along with the main streams[4] gave rise to prolonged argument; and it took eight years of surveys, hearings, and reports before the respective shares of the two countries in the water, the number and situation of gauging stations, the establishment of conservation reservoirs, and the proper operation of the irrigation works on both sides of the line could be defined and provided for. The last order in regard to this problem, which bristled with technical difficulties, was made in 1923.

The Lake of the Woods investigation was undertaken on joint reference of the Governments of Canada and the United States in 1912. It called for the exercise of the powers of investigation and report conferred by Article IX and was, like the matter of the St. Mary and Milk rivers, a task involving technical engineering problems as well as the evaluation of riparian rights. There is accordingly no difficulty in understanding why the commission's final report was not rendered until 1917.

At intervals since 1888, when a dam was constructed in the outlet

4. The commission finally ordered the equal division of those tributaries only which, rising in Saskatchewan, flowed across the boundary. See Order of 1921, in I.J.C. report, *In the Matter . . . of St. Mary and Milk Rivers* (Washington, 1923), p. 3. This was in accordance with the American contention. For a history of the whole dispute and a statement of the points at issue, see Chacko, *op. cit.*, Chap. V.

of the lake at Keewatin, settlers on the Minnesota side had complained of the submergence of their lands. On the other hand there were periods when the levels fell so low that navigation interests were threatened. One of these periods occurred in 1910 and 1911, and the failure of the lake to return to normal levels was attributed by engineers of the War Department of the United States to leakage in the Canadian dam. Meantime plans were being made for a diversion of the waters of Birch Lake, a tributary in Minnesota, from the Lake of the Woods watershed to Lake Superior; and the Canadian Government was opposed to any such diversion on the ground of its threat to navigation in the Lake of the Woods.

What level would best serve all the interests connected with the Lake of the Woods? For navigation, lumbering, and harborage, deep water was needed; while agriculture on the shores demanded low water, as also did the Minnesotan town of Warroad, where drainage and sewage disposal were impeded by high levels. The three questions referred by the Governments to the International Joint Commission in 1912 were, briefly: (1) Is it practicable and desirable to maintain the surface of the lake during the different seasons at a stated level, and if so at what level? (2) What is the extent and value of the lands which would be submerged by such stated level? How can such level be maintained with the least possible damage to all rights and interests, public and private?

Again lengthy hearings, surveys, and engineers' reports were necessary. In 1917 the commission submitted its reply to the reference. It recommended a level between 1,056 and 1,061, sea-level datum. This would entail flooding 23,968 acres in the United States and 40,792 acres in Canada, at a total value of $245,000. The Norman dam in the Winnipeg River was to be used for regulating purposes. To maintain levels in drought periods, use was to be made of existing reservoir capacity on Rainy River and the lakes above Kettle Falls, and as demands for power increased these reservoirs were to be enlarged. The supervision of dams and other apparatus or regulation, indeed the whole work of maintaining the proposed levels was to be committed to an international board of engineers appointed by the two Governments and acting under the International Joint Commission.

The final report led in 1925 to the conclusion of the Lake of the

Woods Treaty and Protocol.[5] These agreements provided for a Canadian Lake of the Woods Control Board to control the outflow from the Lake of the Woods; and an International Lake of the Woods Control Board consisting of two engineers, one appointed by Washington and one by Ottawa, the Canadian engineer to be appointed from among the members of the Canadian Board. The International Board is to determine the rate of outflow whenever the level rises above 1,061 or falls below 1,056, and is also to decide upon the suitability of plans for the enlargement of outlets and construction of protective works. Any disagreement between its members is immediately to be referred to the International Joint Commission, whose decision will be final. Article XI of the treaty establishes the rule that no diversion of waters from the Lake of the Woods watershed to any other watershed shall henceforth be made except with the approval of the International Joint Commission.

The situation in the St. Mary's River, outlet of Lake Superior, was brought before the International Joint Commission by the applications of the Michigan Northern Power Company and the Algoma Steel Corporation in 1913–1914 for approval of the diversion of water and construction of compensating works. The two companies were engaged in power development on the American and Canadian sides of the river, respectively; and the compensating works were designed to offset the large abstraction of water required for their operations. They consisted of a dike with sluice gates stretching from shore to shore, each company undertaking the construction necessary on its side of the boundary line at or near midstream.

Power development on both sides of St. Mary's River had begun in 1888, and the International Waterways Commission established in 1905 had found that control of the discharge from Lake Superior had raised the level of that lake about one foot between 1888 and 1905. This rise had occasioned alarm in property owners and in the many populous municipalities along the shores; while on the other hand the huge navigation interests operating on the lake and

5. *Treaties and Agreements*, pp. 520–524. At the same time an agreement was signed to refer to the I.J.C. for examination and report a similar group of questions regarding the levels of Rainy Lake, Namakan Lake, and neighboring waters. *Ibid.*, pp. 524–525.

through the canals at Sault Ste Marie insisted that any diversion must be offset by a control of the rate of discharge which would prevent lowering, even by a matter of inches, the actual minimum level.

The commission visited the site of the proposed compensating works, heard representations and evidence from all the numerous parties sufficiently concerned to appear at Detroit on March 9 and 10 and at Washington on April 7 and 8, 1914, in response to a general invitation, then, on the basis of a report[6] prepared by Mr. Charles Magrath, one of its Canadian members, declared its conditional approval of the applications on May 26, 1914.

Approval of diversion and remedial works in this case was conditional upon the observance by the two companies of certain rules of construction, operation, and control specified by the commission. These included the establishment of a Board of Control composed of two engineers, one being the officer of the Corps of Engineers charged with the improvement of the Falls of St. Mary's River on the American side and the other an officer appointed by the Canadian Government. To this Board of Control was entrusted the duty of supervising the operation of all the contemplated works, watching the levels recorded, and controlling the amount of water used for power purposes. Any disagreement between its members was to be referred, on application of either Government, to the International Joint Commission for decision.

Part of the reasoning upon which this order was based is particularly important as a guide for subsequent cases. The commission, interpreting the terms of the treaty relating to its jurisdiction and functions, declared that its work was not necessarily finished when it had determined the conditions upon which a diversion or obstruction should be allowed. It might, and in some cases must, retain the right to supervise the way in which these conditions were fulfilled, and to modify, in the light of actual experience, the terms of its order by requiring changes in approved works.[7]

6. *Report in the Matter of the Application of the Michigan Northern Power Company and the Algoma Steel Corporation, Limited* (Washington, Government Printing Office, 1914). This report furnishes, besides an analysis of the interests concerned, a history of the problem.

7. See Mr. Tawney's opinion, *In the Matter of the Application of the Michigan Northern Power Company, Order and Opinion* (Washington, Government Printing Office, 1914), pp. 19–23.

The decision to place the whole project under an international board of control was contrary to the wishes of the United States. The American Government desired to be directly and solely responsible for proper construction and operation of the works on its side of the line. The Dominion of Canada was in favor of international control, and was supported in its stand by the municipal and private interests in both countries. In another matter, the decision ran counter to a proposal in which both Governments joined. The Governments had proposed that differences between members of the Board of Control should be referred to the International Joint Commission for *recommendation;* but the order lays it down that they shall be referred for *decision.* This was because the commission held that to leave the final settlement of such differences to the Governments would risk delay in the protection of vital interests on both sides of the line, and might tend to create, rather than settle differences between the Governments as contemplated in the Boundary Waters Treaty of 1909.[8]

The commission's work on the St. Mary's River applications is an outstanding example at once of sound judicial reasoning and strong, impartial independence. In its assertion of jurisdiction, a matter in which the commission, having regard to the wide purpose which it was designed to accomplish, ought not to be too much restrained by the niceties of legal logic, the order stands in refreshing contrast to the Rainy River decision rendered one year previously. There the applicant company asked for approval of a dam to reach from shore to shore and one of the reasons stated by the commission for dismissing the application was that its competence was limited to cases where an obstruction or diversion on "either side of the line" affected "the natural level or flow of boundary waters on the other side. . . ."[9] The opinion reads:

From a careful examination of these provisions we are unable to find that the two governments intended to confer upon this Commission jurisdiction or control over such an "obstruction" as a dam to be built in boundary waters from shore to shore across the international boundary line as here proposed and we are compelled to hold that as

8. *Ibid.,* pp. 14–17.
9. Boundary Waters Treaty, 1909, Art. 3. *Treaties and Agreements,* pp. 313–314.

the treaty now stands we are under no jurisdictional power to act upon the application before us.

In the Rainy River case the dam was to be the property of one company, though it operated on the Canadian side under Ontario incorporations, and there was legislation by Congress and by the Legislature of Ontario which might be regarded as approaching that special agreement which, by Article III of the Boundary Waters Treaty, would oust the compulsory jurisdiction of the commission. There were, then, distinguishing features, but formally the opinion appears to turn on the fact that the dam was to run all the way across the boundary stream; and that was also true in the St. Mary's River application, though entirely independent companies were responsible for construction on the American and Canadian sides, respectively. Two Canadian Commissioners, Messrs. Powell and Magrath, dissented from the Rainy River opinion; and it must have given them just satisfaction that the reasoning to which they had objected was not brought to bear on the applications of the Michigan Northern Power Company and the Algoma Steel Corporation thirteen months later.

It is not proposed to examine here every matter dealt with by the International Joint Commission. The cases already analyzed are sufficient to show the methods and demonstrate the usefulness of this quasi-judicial, occasionally administrative, and potentially arbitral, body. In all but one case, the commission has hitherto been occupied with questions affecting the level, flow, or purity of boundary waters, and the problems submitted have therefore called for a marked similarity of treatment. This has meant increasing efficiency and confidence, and the notable success achieved has established this institution as a familiar and universally accepted feature of Canadian-American relations. Questions clearly within its competence go to it as a matter of course, and the tendency to appeal to it even when there is doubt upon this head may be expected to grow.[10]

10. Cf. Application of the Greater Winnipeg Water District in 1913 for permission to use the waters of Shoal Lake, connected with the Lake of the Woods. Any doubt as to jurisdiction, this not being boundary water, was settled by adding "and Lake of the Woods"; for at least in some dry years the diversion would affect the quantity of water in the Lake of the Woods. See the "Opinion," *Application of the Greater Winnipeg Water District* (Washington, 1914), p. 3.

There has been some feeling that the dispute in relation to Chicago's diversion from Lake Michigan should have been submitted to this body; but it seems clear that Lake Michigan is not boundary water within the meaning of the treaty, and there have been additional reasons for not invoking the optional arbitral competence of the commission in this matter.[11] Strictly speaking, though its work is often of a judicial nature, the proceedings before it can scarcely be considered arbitrations. Its purpose, which it has admirably accomplished, is to deal with matters involving conflicting interests before they get to the stage of national bitterness.

The one reference not having to do with boundary waters thus far made to the commission was a complaint of the American residents in the Upper Columbia Valley, in the State of Washington, arising out of the damage done to crops by fumes from a sulphuric acid plant operated by the Consolidated Mining and Smelting Company of Canada at Trail, British Columbia. The case will be dealt with in the next section under the heading of "Miscellaneous Claims."

11. See below, pp. 121–124.

CHAPTER V

MISCELLANEOUS CLAIMS

THE HUDSON BAY COMPANY'S CLAIMS, 1869

THE Oregon Treaty of 1846 made provision in its second, third, and fourth articles, for the protection of the rights of the Hudson Bay Company, and its subsidiary the Puget's Sound Agricultural Company, in the territory along the Columbia conceded to the United States. Article II preserved to the company and to all British subjects trading with it free navigation of the Columbia "on the same footing as citizens of the United States." Article III promised that "the possessory rights of the Hudson's Bay Company, and of all British subjects who may be already in the occupation of land or other property lawfully acquired within the said territory, shall be respected." Article IV laid it down that:

The farms, lands and other property of every description, belonging to the Puget's Sound Agricultural Company, on the north side of the Columbia River, shall be confirmed to the said Company. In case, however, the situation of those farms and lands should be considered by the United States to be of public and political importance, and the United States Government should signify a desire to obtain possession of the whole or any part thereof, the property so required shall be transferred to the said government at a proper valuation, to be agreed upon between the Parties.

Before 1846 the Hudson Bay Company had been the principal power in the Oregon territory. It had a trading monopoly hardly less effective in practice against American citizens than it was in law and in fact against British subjects; and such order as existed was maintained by its government. After the Oregon Treaty its position rapidly deteriorated. Settlers squatted on its lands, shot its cattle, and dispossessed it of its trading stations. The application of United States revenue laws to goods brought in through the Columbia for trading purposes rendered nugatory the right of navigation.

The company applied from time to time to the British Government and through it to the Government of the United States for the enforcement of the treaty and the redress of wrongs already suffered. The United States, taking the view that its obligations were fulfilled if the company's property and rights were not officially taken away and if recourse to the ordinary courts were open to the applicant, took no steps to afford any special protection. The company, despairing of its prospects in the Oregon, offered to sell out to the United States. At one time one million dollars was offered on behalf of the United States, at another the company was willing to accept five hundred thousand. The two sides, however, failed to agree at any one time on terms of transfer and surrender, and the succession of trespass and complaint dragged on until 1863. In that year a treaty to arbitrate the whole matter was concluded at Washington.

Under this arrangement of 1863, all claims of the two companies with respect to their possessory rights were to "be settled by the transfer of those rights and claims to the Government of the United States for an adequate money consideration." Great Britain and the United States each appointed a commissioner and the two commissioners were instructed to choose an umpire. In the event of their failure to concur in this matter, the King of Italy was to be invited to make the choice. It will be seen that a method was being adopted which had been used in the St. Croix River arbitration in 1798 and in the London Commission of 1853. In the present case, the two commissioners were able as had happened in the earlier instance, to agree on the umpire, and recourse to the King of Italy was therefore unnecessary. What is more remarkable is that they were eventually able to reach an accord upon the substance of the dispute without the casting vote of their umpire.

The aggregate claims of the Hudson Bay and Puget's Sound companies amounted to nearly five and a half million dollars. This amount was arrived at by a computation not only of the properties and rights now being transferred or surrendered but of damages previously suffered owing to the failure of the United States to fulfil its obligations under the treaty of 1846. The sum upon which the commissioners finally agreed as full compensation was six hundred and fifty thousand dollars, or about one ninth that claimed. They had struck out the item of claim touching the navigation of the Columbia, valued by the Company at $1,460,000, on the ground that their terms of reference limited them to questions arising out of Articles III and IV of the treaty of 1846, whereas the right of navigation resulted from Article II of that instrument. Even so, the disparity is a striking one, in spite of the familiar practice of plaintiffs to ask for a great deal more than they hope to receive. Yet the British Commissioner did not find the difference too outrageous; and there was no room in this case for Canadian complaint that legitimate interests were being sacrificed by English representatives for the sake of harmony between the Mother Country and the United States. For even if Canadians had been disposed to take up the cudgels for an English company, they would have been checked here by the fact that the British Commissioner was himself a Canadian, none other than Sir John Rose.

Sir John's reasoning on the subject of compensation is worth quoting as an instance of the common sense and evenness of judgment so essential in an arbiter.

It is obvious that in a case of this nature, where there is ground for much honest difference of opinion . . . , each Commissioner must be prepared to make some concession in the views he holds, if a common judgment is to be reached. There is no rule by which the testimony can be appreciated, to warrant the conclusion that a positive sum—no more and no less—is made out in proof. . . .

My individual opinion would have been in favour of awarding a considerably larger sum to the Claimants, than that in which my colleague is willing to concur. Yet the inherent difficulties of the case . . . would seem to impose on one seeking to perform his judicial functions with impartiality, and to accomplish effectual results, the duty of not pushing to the limit of irreconcilable difference the opinion he holds; but on the contrary of modifying his views to some extent within the range to which the testimony may reasonably be held to apply, where he finds an honest opinion equally strong, adverse to his.[1]

The American Commissioner had estimated the compensation due at a smaller figure than that adopted in the award. He also, therefore, had made concessions, and upon much the same reasoning as his Canadian colleague. In his "Opinion," after frankly admitting that the respect actually paid to the rights of the companies as defined in the treaty of 1846 had been "scarcely commensurate with the

1. Moore, *History and Digest,* I, 255–256.

extent of the obligations of the Government of the United States," he writes:

From a mere trifle on the one side, all the way to the enormous sum demanded by the Claimants' memorial on the other, almost any sum could be supported by testimony free from criticism affecting either the fidelity or intelligence of the witnesses. . . . I could not feel so sure of the absolute correctness of my own valuation, as to warrant me in refusing to yield in the direction of his strong convictions, within what I conceived to be the limits of my possible error, especially as I found him not unwilling, on his part, to give due weight to the like considerations.[2]

One feature of this case was the elaborate nature of the preparation necessary for adequate presentation. The process of collecting evidence lasted from May, 1865, to April, 1869, and touched in its range England, British Columbia, Washington Territory, the states of Oregon, New York, Pennsylvania, Ohio, Michigan, Tennessee, North Carolina, Louisiana, and Florida, and the city of Washington. The objects of inquiry were of course the actual facts as to the holdings and rights of the two companies and their economic value. Evidence was taken in all the places mentioned under regulations that required reasonable notice from one party to the other, examination and cross-examination, and the recording of voluminous depositions. This was the task of counsel for the companies on the one side and for the United States on the other. It was accomplished with great pains and thoroughness. The dossiers finally submitted to the commissioners in April, 1869, comprised some 2,500 pages, but they were able in September of the same year to render their award.

CLAIMS SCHEDULED UNDER THE AGREEMENT OF 1910

In 1910, Great Britain and the United States made provision to arbitrate an accumulation of grievances going back as far as 1811. The agreement opens with a preamble reciting that both countries are signatories of the Hague Convention of 1907 for the Pacific Settlement of International Disputes, and proceeds to adopt not only the mechanism of that convention for setting up a tribunal but

2. Moore, *op. cit.,* I, 261–262.

its regulations for the conduct of cases submitted. This, in spite of the fact that Great Britain had not then, and has not since, ratified the convention of 1907.

Each party was to present its claims to the other within four months of confirmation of the agreement. The claims so presented were to be arbitrated provided both parties agreed that they should. Either party might reserve a claim for further examination. All claims presented and not reserved were to be grouped in one or more schedules, each schedule to be agreed on by the United States with consent of the Senate, and His Majesty's Government reserving the right to obtain the concurrence of the self-governing Dominions in the inclusion of any claim affecting their interests.

All claims outstanding on August 18, 1910, and not so presented and scheduled or reserved were declared to be finally barred.

The tribunal was established in the manner set out in Article 87 of the Hague convention of 1907, each of the parties appointing an arbiter and these two choosing an umpire. It began its work in 1913 and completed the first schedule submitted to it in 1926. The total of British claims in this schedule was 59 (one of which was withdrawn), and of American claims 41. The tribunal gave 28 decisions in favor of Great Britain and 71 in favor of the United States. In geographical origin the cases ranged from the Philippines, through North America, to South Africa; but the majority of them were complaints of American citizens against the authorities in Canada and Newfoundland, or of Canadians against the authorities of the United States.

Of the principal cases in which Canada was concerned some will be found sufficiently summarized in a later chapter.[3] Others, more interesting for the facts than for the questions of law involved, are now to be examined.

The *Lord Nelson*

The *Lord Nelson*[4] was a British schooner seized by the naval authorities of the United States on Lake Ontario in June, 1812, about two weeks before the outbreak of war. She was sold by decree of the

3. See below, pp. 79–92.
4. Fred K. Nielsen, *American and British Claims Arbitration* (Washington, Government Printing Office, 1926), pp. 432–435.

Federal District Court and the proceeds paid into court; but in 1817 the same tribunal declared the capture illegal and ordered the sale price, about $3,000, to be handed over to the owners. This money having been embezzled by the clerk of the Court, the order was not carried out.

On February 3, 1819, the British Government presented on behalf of the owners a claim to the United States for indemnity. This was repeated on several occasions, and bills were introduced in Congress to authorize payment; but no payment was made. In 1837, the Secretary of the Navy, on instructions from Congress, reported that the true value of the ship at capture was $5,000; but in 1914 no satisfaction had yet been given and the case came before the Pecuniary Claims Tribunal.

The United States admitted liability to the extent of $5,000, but Great Britain claimed interest on this sum from the date of capture. The terms of submission annexed to the Agreement of 1910 (Section IV) laid it down that interest might be allowed only from the date when the claim was first brought to the notice of the other party, and at a rate not exceeding 4 per cent.

The tribunal declared two generally recognized rules of international law applicable to such claims. The first was that "in case of wrongful possession and use, the amount of indemnity awarded must represent both the value of the property taken and the value of its use"; the second that "interest is to be paid at the rate current in the place and at the time the principal was due." Here, however, the parties had by specific agreement limited the rate. They had moreover designated a *dies a quo* for the accrual of interest. Accordingly, though it would otherwise have been justifiable to allow interest from the date of capture, and at the rate current in North America in 1812, the tribunal awarded the maximum agreed rate (4 per cent) from February 3, 1819, when Great Britain first presented its claim.

THE *Wanderer, Favourite, Kate, Jessie, Thomas F. Bayard,* AND *Pescawha*[5]

These were all cases where Canadian vessels were seized or interfered with while engaged in sealing operations in the North Pacific

5. *Ibid.,* pp. 459–482, 515–519.

Ocean. In all of them, the action of the American officers was found unjustified and the liability of their Government to compensation affirmed by the tribunal. The *Wanderer* and the *Favourite* (1894) were seized for having a shotgun each and ammunition on board, whereas the agreed regulations following the award of the Behring Sea Arbitration in 1893 forbade only the use of such weapons. The *Kate* (1896) was seized because she had on board two sealskins bearing evidence of having been shot in Behring Sea. The others (1909) had their guns put under seal while hunting sea otters, though there was no authorization in the agreed regulations to do this specific thing.

The general principle asserted by the tribunal as governing these claims was that, except by special convention, any interference by a cruiser with a foreign vessel pursuing a lawful avocation on the high seas in time of peace is unwarranted and illegal; and that every special convention, being an agreed exception to the rule, must be strictly construed. The *bona fides* of officials who overstep the strict limits of such conventions is no defense for their governments against a claim for resulting damage.

Compensation was awarded after a careful estimate in each case of loss suffered by the vessel by reason of her detention. This involved detailed calculations of the average daily catch of seals and the average value of skins. Such methods are at best imperfect, but certainly the tribunal did not err on the side of lavishness.

THE *David J. Adams*[6]

This was one of the large group of claims put forward by the United States in respect of the seizure of fishing vessels in alleged violation of the treaty of 1818. The master of the *Adams* had been purchasing bait in Digby Basin, and the schooner, seized on May 7, 1886, was condemned and sold by order of the Vice-Admiralty Court at Halifax in 1889.

The first line of argument adopted by the United States was that the phrase "American fishermen shall be admitted to enter such bays or harbours for the purpose of shelter and of repairing damages therein, of purchasing wood, and of obtaining water, and for no

6. Nielsen, *op. cit.,* pp. 524–536.

other purpose whatever" in Article I of the treaty of 1818, imposed a positive obligation to admit American vessels for the four purposes specified, but did not prohibit entry for other purposes. Entry for other purposes might be prohibited by British legislation, but did not become unlawful until so prohibited. The tribunal held that even if this very doubtful interpretation were correct, the prohibition of entry for other purposes was contained in the British Act of 1819 (59 Geo. III, c. 36, s. 3).

This holding was met by the interesting contention that the prohibition had rarely been enforced, and that

where for a long continued period a government has, either contrary to its laws or without having any laws in force covering the case, permitted to aliens a certain course of action, it cannot under the principles of international law, suddenly change that course and make it affect those aliens already engaged in forbidden transactions as the result of that course and deprive aliens of their property so acquired, without rendering themselves liable to an international reclamation.

To accept this argument would have been to admit that a servitude can be acquired by prescription even against the explicit statutory law of the servient State. It does not appear from the report that the arbiters had this consideration in mind. They merely declared it difficult to apply "a principle based upon the *bona fides* of foreigners" to a case where the master had acted in conscious violation of Canadian law and his owner's instructions. The claim was accordingly disallowed; but in view of the fact that forfeiture for the purchase of bait was first enacted by the Act of 1886 (49 Vict. c. 114) which was later than the seizure of the *Adams*, and in consideration of the innocence and poverty of the owner, the tribunal urged the British Government to compensate him, as an act of grace, for his loss.

THE *Tattler*[7]

Of the two claims concerning the *Tattler*, one will be dealt with in another connection.[8] The second arose out of the seizure of this schooner at North Sydney and her detention for three days on the ground that she had shipped men from a Canadian port without the

7. *Ibid.*, pp. 489–494.   8. Below, pp. 90–91.

license required by 55–56 Victoria, c. 3. These events took place in 1905, and the claim, which came before the Pecuniary Claims Tribunal in 1920, was for $2,100 with interest.

The shipping of men without the required license was admitted. It was clear from the evidence, however, that the master had properly applied for such license and that his application had been wrongfully refused by the Canadian authorities. The tribunal held the British Government (that being formally the party before it) responsible for the detention in spite of the fact that the *Tattler* had committed acts illegal under Canadian law. "It is difficult," the award runs, "to admit that a foreign ship may be seized for not having a certain document when the document has been refused to it by the very authorities who required that it should be obtained."

Of special importance is the tribunal's treatment of the *quantum* of damages. The owners claimed the value of 665 barrels of herring not caught because of the three days' detention. No evidence was, however, produced to show the likelihood of such a catch, and the arbiters very properly insisted upon reasonable substantiation of the amount of loss. The facts established justified an award of only $630, a sum arrived at after consideration of the length of detention, tonnage, equipment, and manning of the vessel.

This does not mean that the tribunal was unwilling to enter upon a calculation of the value of the probable catch. With exactly the same personnel, it made such calculation a year later in the *Wanderer, Kate,* etc.[9] But apparently it was not furnished in the present instance with the elements upon which to base a reasonably accurate estimate of *lucrum cessans.*

Yukon Lumber Company

Judging by Mr. Nielsen's reports, a number of British claims were badly, and one, the Cadenhead case, offensively, presented. Perhaps the worst exhibition of ineptitude is provided by the claim for Crown dues on certain lumber cut in Canadian territory, sold by the cutter to a contractor, and by him to the American military authority in Alaska. Great Britain demanded alternatively the dues or the value of the timber from the United States. The amount of

9. Above, pp. 65–66.

dues involved, some $200, was so small that it should never have formed the object of a claim between governments. The tribunal very properly pointed out that the alternatives were contradictory, the claim for dues admitting passage of the property and excluding any case for recovery. If the matter was to be pressed against the United States at all, it should have been pressed as a claim for repossession or its equivalent. Unfortunately the Crown agent had never attempted to recover the timber from the cutter or contractor, but had demanded only the stumpage dues. The grievance now complained of could easily have been avoided, even after this stage, by asking the Alaskan military authority to stop payment until the dues had been discharged. Failure to take either of these opportunities was held by the arbiters tantamount to ratification of the trespass of unlicensed cutting; and they refused to admit that after thirteen years of such ratification the British Government could now assert ownership. They applied, without explicitly mentioning it, the doctrine of estoppel.

As for the stumpage dues, the tribunal observed that the United States military authorities had purchased the timber in good faith from the contractor, had no notice of its origin, and did not in any way assume the engagements of the original cutter toward the Canadian Government. If the law of Canada gave the Crown a lien for unpaid dues, this could not operate against a foreigner on lumber now outside Canadian territory unless provided for by the law of the foreign country. In any event the lumber was now state property and not subject to seizure.

This case has some value as an application of estoppel between States and also for its observation on the limits of liens established by foreign municipal law. The practical lesson is, however, perhaps its most valuable contribution. The record suggests very forcibly that items to be included in schedules for international arbitration should be carefully scrutinized to make certain that the pecuniary or political importance of the claim merits such serious treatment. It suggests secondly that, if a claim deserves to be made an issue between States, it also deserves careful and competent analysis, preparation, and presentation. Failure to observe these cardinal rules is a slight to the dignity of the arbitral tribunal and is apt, even, to bring contempt upon the practice of arbitration.

THE TRAIL SMELTER

FOR some years prior to 1927 the inhabitants of Stevens County in the State of Washington had been complaining of damage to forests, crops, and soils from the fumes issuing from the plant of the Consolidated Mining and Smelting Company at Trail, British Columbia. The plant was situated within a few miles of the border and the fumes, containing a high proportion of sulphur dioxide, drifted down the Columbia Valley to the increasing detriment of agricultural interests in American territory. In 1927 the Government of the United States proposed reference to the International Joint Commission for investigation and report under Article IX of the Boundary Waters Treaty of 1909. The Canadian Government agreed and the matter was duly referred in August, 1928. Technical experts for both Governments and for the company carried out tests of soils, foliage, and vegetation in the area, their findings were incorporated in the opposing briefs, and they were orally examined by the commission. Hearings were held at Northport in the State of Washington, at Nelson in British Columbia, and at Washington, D. C. These extended from October, 1928, to February, 1930, and the report of the commission was signed at Toronto on February 28, 1931.

The reference to the commission took the form of five questions touching (1) the extent of the damage to property in the State of Washington; (2) the indemnity for damage done; (3) the probable effect in the State of Washington of future operations of the smelter; (4) the method of providing indemnity for future damages; and (5) any other phase of the problem on which the commission thought it proper or necessary to make recommendations.

The report dated February 28, 1931, was accompanied by a map showing the geographical extent of damage. On the question of indemnity, the sum of $350,000 was set as covering all past damage and all damage up to and including January 1, 1932. As to the probable effect of future operations, the commission held that, if the company completed its plan of sulphuric-acid works to reduce the sulphur content of the smelter fumes in accordance with the commission's recommendations, the damage would be greatly reduced if not eliminated by the end of 1931. In the event, however, of complaints being made after that date, the commission recommended that any claims not adjusted by the company within a reasonable time should be examined by the two Governments, and that the amount of compensation by them found due should be immediately paid by the company. Under part five of its terms of reference, the commission set out in detail the measures which it believed would eliminate the injurious elements in the fumes issuing from the company's smelters. It recommended that the application of these measures should be supervised by scientists appointed by and reporting to both Governments, that the Government of the United States should be free to take up with the Government of Canada any question as to the company's diligence in proceeding with the necessary works, and that the company's report that it had completed these works should be subject to joint confirmation by the American and Canadian authorities.

The Trail Smelter case gave the International Joint Commission its first opportunity to demonstrate its usefulness in a conflict of interest not connected with boundary waters. The final report—and it must be remembered that the commission was not called upon to render a decision—obviously leaves ample room for future differences between the Governments, to whom is committed the task of seeing that its recommendations are actually carried out. But the submission of the complaints brought about at least a temporary pacification of feeling, and there is every ground for hope that the loyal enforcement of the measures approved by the commission will put an end to a situation which had become a cause of acute friction.

THE *VINCES*, *MAZEL TOV*, *I'M ALONE*, ETC.

THE régime of Prohibition in the United States, and the highly organized activities of liquor smugglers employing vessels of Canadian registry for the importation of intoxicating liquors into the United States in violation of the laws of that country, gave rise to numerous disputes as to the limits of jurisdiction in coastal waters. Some of these were settled by diplomatic agents, some went to Courts of the United States, and one to a special commission set up as described in the following paragraph.

A treaty of 1924[10] gave to the United States the right to search

10. *Treaties and Agreements,* pp. 509–511.

and, in the presence of reasonable cause, to seize, vessels under the British flag suspected of importing alcoholic beverages into the United States, provided, however, that this right should not be exercised at a greater distance from the coast than could be traversed in one hour by the suspected vessel. Any claim arising out of the improper exercise of this right was to be referred to a commission of two persons, one nominated by Great Britain, one by the United States. If the commissioners failed to agree upon a joint report, the claim was to be submitted to the Pecuniary Claims Tribunal established under the Agreement of 1910.[11]

American Coast Guard officials, acting under Federal legislation which authorized them to apprehend ships at a distance of twelve miles from shore, in a number of instances exceeded the limit of one hour's steaming imposed by the treaty. In one such case,[12] that of the *Mazel Tov*, a Canadian rumrunner, which had been boarded and seized 11½ miles out though she was not capable of more than 10 miles per hour, the Supreme Court of the United States in January, 1933, disallowed the seizure, on the ground that

the Treaty, being later in date than the Act of 1922, superseded, so far as inconsistent with the terms of the Act, the authority which had been conferred by §581 upon Officers of the Coast Guard to board, search and seize beyond our territorial waters. . . . The Treaty was not abrogated by re-enacting §581 in the Tariff Act of 1930 in the identical terms of the Act of 1922. A treaty will not be deemed to have been abrogated or modified by a later statute unless such purpose on the part of Congress has been clearly expressed.

This judgment overrules the main grounds of decision in *Gillam* v. *United States*, 1928, where the seizure of the *Vinces* more than twelve miles from shore was upheld by the Circuit Court of Appeals. Parker, Circuit Judge, had there held that the statute of 1922 was valid and not modified by the treaty of 1924. There was, however, an alternative ground in the doctrine of hot pursuit, since the chase had started within an hour's steaming distance of shore. The judgment shows clearly that Judge Parker considered this doctrine applicable

11. See above, pp. 63–64.
12. *Cook* v. *U.S.A.*, Supreme Court Reports, October Term, 1932, pp. 641 *seq.*

both for the purposes of the tariff act with its twelve-mile limit and for the purposes of the treaty.[13]

National courts are bound, in the prevailing theory, to enforce their national statutes irrespective of international law, and the decisive factor for the Supreme Court was that the treaty of 1924 was of the same force as a statute. An international tribunal, dealing with similar disputes, would have been bound to hold the national law limited, not merely by treaty, but also by the common law of nations. Until the theory of the supremacy of national law is reversed—a consummation which, however devoutly to be wished, is probably far distant—a wider understanding of this difference between national and international tribunals would serve a useful purpose. It would diminish the expectation of objective justice when cases involving international interests come before national courts and alleviate the indignation which follows decisions that ignore the law of nations.

The only dispute referred to a commission as provided in the treaty of 1924 was that concerning the *I'm Alone*. It will be necessary in a later portion of this essay[14] to state the facts in some detail and to analyze the law involved. Some external aspects of the case are, however, worthy of notice here.

The *I'm Alone*, a schooner of Canadian register, admittedly engaged in the business of smuggling liquor into the United States, was sunk in 1929 by a vessel of the United States Coast Guard more than two hundred miles out to sea. The cargo was of course lost, the master and crew lost their personal effects, and one sailor was drowned.

The sympathy felt in Canada for the hardships inflicted on Canadians engaged in the profitable violation of the Prohibition laws of the United States had always been somewhat surprisingly widespread and vocal. This instance of supreme violence roused a great many sober citizens who had hitherto taken little part in the recriminations against American officials. Something approaching a general outcry resounded through the press and from public platforms from one side of the Dominion to the other. For days the *I'm Alone* was

13. 27 *Federal Reporter*, 2d series, pp. 296 *seq.*
14. Below, pp. 93–96.

"front-page news," and many editorials[15] were written and at least one sermon preached in condemnation of the ruthless measures employed by agents of the United States in their attempt to enforce a law which was described as bad in itself and to which, in any event, Canadians owed no respect.

Great publicity was given to the steps taken by the Canadian Legation at Washington to ascertain the true facts, to convince the State Department that the sinking of the *I'm Alone* was a violation of international law and of the Liquor Treaty of 1924, and to obtain redress. Questions were asked in Parliament, and all the other signs of general indignation were manifest. The agitation only began to die down when steps were taken by the two Governments to refer the incident to two commissioners to be appointed as provided in Article IV of the 1924 treaty. The tranquillizing effect of that decision bears eloquent witness to the value of arbitral arrangements made in advance for the disposal of possible disputes.

The proposal to arbitrate came in this instance from the United States. It was made on April 17, 1929, and accepted by the Canadian Minister at Washington on behalf of his Government on April 24.[16] The commission was duly appointed, but the original Canadian member died before the preliminary investigations were complete and his place was taken by the Chief Justice of Canada. A period of almost six years was taken up with the preparation of the briefs on both sides, the exchange of written cases, and the hearings of oral argument. In spite of this long delay, the fact that the whole matter was under joint judicial consideration removed it from the domain of public controversy, and it is safe to say that it had passed from the memory of most people before the final decision was rendered.

The commissioners made a joint interim report on June 30, 1933, stating their opinion that "the admittedly intentional sinking of the suspected vessel was not justified by anything in the Convention" (of 1924), but recommending that the agents of the two Governments prepare and submit to the commission the contentions of their

15. A sober, though acrid, expression of Canadian feeling may be found in the leading editorial, *Montreal Gazette,* April 9, 1929, p. 12.

16. *Claim of the British Ship "I'm Alone," Documents* (King's Printer, Ottawa, 1935), pp. 32–50. The commissioners' interim and final reports are both reproduced in this publication.

Governments regarding the ultimate beneficial interest in the vessel and cargo and a joint statement, or separate statements, of the sums which should be payable by the United States if the commission should determine that compensation was due.

The interim report disposed of the main case of the United States. American counsel had argued that the action of the Coast Guard vessel was no more than the necessities of law enforcement demanded in the circumstances and that the distance from shore was immaterial because the pursuit had begun within one hour's distance of shore[17] and had been uninterruptedly sustained up to the moment of sinking. The commissioners held that even if the right of hot pursuit were assumed, a matter on which they were not agreed, the sinking of the schooner was not an unavoidable incident of the exercise of rights granted by the treaty. This left only the question of compensation. In its final report, dated January 5, 1935, the commission denied compensation to the owners of the ship and cargo on the ground that, notwithstanding Canadian incorporation, the beneficial owners were, with one possible exception, American citizens joined in a conspiracy to violate the law of their country. Substantial indemnities were, however, awarded to the Canadian Government for the master and crew and for the widow of the drowned man. In addition, the commissioners recommended an apology by the United States to the Canadian Government, coupled with the payment of $25,000 as a material amend in respect of the wrong. These recommendations were observed to the letter.

In the *I'm Alone*, as in some other incidents arising out of the enforcement of the Prohibition law in the United States, Canada was officially in the position of protecting persons who had set out deliberately to make profit by the systematic violation of the laws of a friendly neighboring country. As it stands at present, international law gives to State A a clear right to intervene when the agents of State B interfere with the non-piratical activities of the subjects of State A on the high seas. A fanatical devotion to the corollaries of sovereignty, still apparent in the practice of States, makes this right a jealously guarded treasure; and we shall probably have to witness, for a long time to come, the employment of all the machinery

17. On the admissibility of the doctrine of hot pursuit in treaty extensions of territorial jurisdiction, see below, pp. 80–81.

of diplomacy and arbitration for the protection of persons engaged in undertakings which, from the international point of view, are undeniably antisocial. The withdrawal of national protection in such cases would be a long step toward the achievement of a real international community.

CHAPTER VI

CONTRIBUTIONS TO INTERNATIONAL LAW AND PROCEDURE

OUT of the American Revolution and the consequent division of North America between Great Britain and the United States came the modern revival and generalization of arbitration. That practice, already employed by the Greek cities of antiquity, and again surprisingly frequent in the stormy Middle Ages, had gone out of fashion in the fifteenth century.[1] True, it did not disappear completely, but its modern use as a normal method of settling disputes that defy the powers of diplomatic negotiation dates from the Jay Treaty of 1794. In his book, *Une Cour de Justice Internationale*,[2] published by the Carnegie Foundation in 1918, Dr. James Brown Scott has studied the external circumstances and personal influences to which we owe that development of recourse to judicial settlement wherein lies the world's best hope for peace. It will be sufficient here merely to mention this general contribution of British-American and Canadian-American relations to international politics before passing on to the analysis of particular rules and methods which have been suggested or reënforced by the proceedings and decisions of our arbitral commissions.

THE RESPONSIBILITY OF STATES FOR WRONGS DONE TO ALIENS

THE conditions and measure of a State's responsibility for injuries to the person or property of aliens are still one of the least settled and definite chapters of international law. The codification conference assembled by the League of Nations at The Hague in 1930 failed, in spite of long and elaborate preparation, to agree on a solution of any one of the numerous problems with which the topic

1. See Novacovitch, *Les Compromis et les arbitrages internationaux du XIIe au XVe siècle* (Paris, 1905), and the summary in Christian L. Lange, *Histoire de l'internationalisme* (New York, 1919).
2. See particularly pp. 165–174.

bristles. Knowing this, we cannot hope to find categorical answers to these problems in the history of Canadian-American arbitration, or even in the broader material of British-American disputes. What we do find is useful juristic analysis of the rights of aliens and corresponding duties of the State, and the equitable application of general principles to specific cases. The decisions reached, moreover, and even the *obiter dicta* with which they are accompanied, furnish precedents or guidance which will go on influencing the settlement of similar issues. For arbitration loves precedent and example hardly less than does the common law; and the citation of awards and the borrowing of judicial reasoning from analogous cases constitute, with the invocation of doctrinal authority, striking features of arbitral practice between British countries and the United States.

These observations do not of course imply that either the decisions themselves or the published *rationes decidendi* are, or should be, binding. We shall find matter for criticism. But the presence of believed error does not mean that a particular adjudication on a vexed question may not assist materially in the development of a consistent jurisprudence. The case at least affords practical testing ground for abstract principle.

TERRITORIAL LIMITS TO THE ADMINISTRATIVE ACTION OF STATES

The fundamental principle of the international maritime law is that no nation can exercise a right of visitation and search over foreign vessels pursuing a lawful avocation on the high seas, except in time of war or by special agreement. . . . Any such agreement, being an exception to the general principle, must be construed *stricto jure* [*sic*].[3]

The same principle had determined the awards in the *Argus* and the *Washington*, seized on the open sea and in the Bay of Fundy, respectively, for alleged violation of the Fisheries Treaty of 1818. The offenders there were British cruisers enforcing the exclusion of American fishing vessels from waters in which the United States was believed to have renounced by the treaty the right to fish. These cruisers were operating under the Nova Scotia Hovering Act of 1836, which proceeded on the theory that Fundy was a British bay.

3. The *Wanderer,* F. K. Nielsen, *American and British Claims Arbitration,* p. 462. See above, pp. 65–66.

In 1920 the British-American Pecuniary Claims Tribunal decided against the United States a dispute arising out of the application of American "Hovering Acts." The *Coquitlam* was a British ship owned by the Union Steamships Company, of British Columbia. She was condemned in 1893 by the District Court of Alaska for having, in violation of United States statutes, delivered supplies to, and received sealskins from, schooners in the North Pacific within four leagues from the American coast. The decree was reversed by the United States Circuit Court of Appeals, but the claim of the owners and charterers for damages arising out of the seizure went unsatisfied and after long delay came before the tribunal established by the Agreement of 1910.[4]

In behalf of the Canadian vessel it was contended that the "Hovering Acts" could not legally be enforced against foreign craft outside the three-mile belt. As, however, the Circuit Court of Appeals had decided that, quite apart from this consideration, the *Coquitlam* had committed no offense contemplated in the relevant statutes, it was unnecessary to deal with this aspect of the case. The American defense before the tribunal was that the revenue officers had acted in good faith and with probable cause, and that there was consequently no liability for resulting damages. It is regrettable that the tribunal should have thought it necessary to enter into such a question as probable cause. The case presented an excellent opportunity to reject once and for all defenses of this nature. A national court had held that the seizure was wrongful. The tribunal was convinced that damage had ensued. The notion that any further element, such as bad faith or absence of probable cause, need be present to create liability on the part of the State should have been emphatically repudiated. The tribunal's citation of Chief Justice Marshall's definition of probable cause, and its very flimsy distinction between doubt as to the existence of facts and doubt as to their wrongful character, were precisely the sort of reasoning which adds to the confusion of thought surrounding public responsibility in tort. On any true analysis, moreover, good faith implies probable cause, and the tribunal had already held that the good faith of public officers did not exonerate the United States.

4. Nielsen, *op. cit.,* pp. 445 *seq.*

One of the most ingenious efforts made in recent times to extend the competence of the State over wide expanses of ocean was the argument, advanced by American counsel and accepted by the American members of the tribunal, that the United States had a right of ownership or at least of protection in the fur seals of Behring Sea. The contention was based primarily on the Roman law regarding animals *ferae naturae* exhibiting an *animus revertendi*, as it is laid down in the Institutes of Justinian, 2, 1, 15. This rule gave property in peafowl, pigeons, and deer which, though they range far, return habitually to dovecot or private park. The British counter case, and Sir Charles Russell in oral argument, objected to the application of this principle to migratory animals spending half their life in one place and half in another. "The fur seal might as truly be said to have the *animus revertendi* to the ocean as to the Pribilof Islands."[5] Moreover, the *animus revertendi*, to operate as a basis for title, must have been induced by the industry of man. Perhaps, however, the consideration which had most weight in causing the majority of the tribunal to reject the American reasoning was the extent to which it might be pushed. How distinguish, indeed, the case of fish returning to banks or rivers, or of birds periodically visiting feeding or breeding grounds?

In all of these cases the government whose officials had carried their duties beyond the three-mile limit, and beyond the bounds of any treaty extending that limit for special purposes, was held liable to compensate the alien who had suffered damage. It is perhaps worth further emphasis that the good faith of an official so acting does not negative his government's responsibility. *Bona fides*, it is pointed out in the *Wanderer*, and in the *Jessie, Thomas F. Bayard*, and *Pascawha*,[6] may excuse an official vis-à-vis the national authority; but that authority is liable to other states for errors in judgment committed by its agents within the scope of their duties.

Hot pursuit. One extension of police competence beyond the three-mile limit is pretty generally recognized under the heading of "hot pursuit." Where an offense has been committed and pursuit begun

5. Moore, *op. cit.*, p. 881.
6. Nielsen, *op. cit.*, pp. 462, 465–466, and 480–481. Cf. the *Coquitlam*, above, p. 79.

within territorial waters, the offending vessel may be seized at any distance before she enters the maritime belt of another state.[7] Special treaties have been concluded, notably between the United States under the régime of Prohibition and other Powers whose ships entered American ports with alcoholic liquors on board, extending for specified purposes the margin within which foreign vessels might be searched and seized. The question has arisen whether the right of hot pursuit can be claimed under such treaties without explicit provision in their text. Do these treaties, in other words, legalize by implication a seizure effected outside the limits set by their clauses if pursuit has begun inside those limits? An affirmative answer seems to violate the constantly enunciated principle that agreements extending national competence beyond the bounds set by international law are to be interpreted *stricto sensu*, because they restrict the liberty and encroach upon the sovereignty of other States.[8] Yet the affirmative view was adopted, at least as an alternative ground of decision, in the case of the *Vinces*, by the United States Circuit Court of Appeals in 1928.[9] The *Vinces* was a schooner of Canadian ownership seized by the American Coast Guard more than twelve miles out after a chase which began seven and a half miles, or within one hour's sailing distance, from shore; and the seizure was upheld by the Court.

The same question presented itself in the *I'm Alone*,[10] and in their interim report the American and Canadian commissioners stated that they were not yet in agreement upon the point. As, however, they had already decided that the sinking of the vessel was unjustified, even if the right of hot pursuit were assumed, it was not necessary that they should agree; and their final report treats the matter of hot pursuit as not "now material."[11]

7. See, for example, Oppenheim, *International Law*, I, 496.

8. The Helsingfors Convention of 1925, by which eleven Baltic states extend their marginal belt for the purpose of preventing smuggling, specifically admits hot pursuit. De Martens, *Nouveau Recueil Général de Traités*, series III, Vol. 20, pp. 131 *seq.*

9. *Gillam* v. *U.S.*, 27 *Federal Reporter*, 2d series, 296 *seq.* For comment see 26 *Michigan Law Review*, 551 *seq.*

10. See above, pp. 73–75.

11. The two reports are reprinted in 29 *A.J.I.L.*, 326 *seq.*

LIMITS TO THE RIGHTS OF ALIENS

The claims of certain Canadian exporters of hay demanding the refund of excessive customs duties paid to United States collectors were among those that fell to be decided by the British-American tribunal set up under the treaty of 1910.[12] The duties were paid between 1868 and 1882. In 1882 a firm of commission merchants in New York, who had paid similar duties, instituted proceedings by notice to the collector, appeal to the Secretary of the Treasury, and recourse to the courts, for the recovery of 10 of the 20 per cent ad valorem which they had been charged. Their mode of procedure was that laid down by law for such protests, and they succeeded in their action. Hearing of this, our Canadian exporters began in 1883 to press through diplomatic channels a demand to the same effect. The Secretary of the Treasury took the ground that no refund was due to anyone who had failed within the time allowed to institute the proceedings required by statute, and the tribunal, deciding the case in 1925, forty-two years after the claim had first been presented, upheld this contention.

This was a clear instance of asking for an alien privileges which would not have been granted to a national, and the upshot of the tribunal's remarks is that such a claim cannot succeed. The arbitrators said:

It is of course conceivable that a statutory procedure might be so unreasonable as effectually to deny the right of protest and appeal, but we do not find any such condition here; and even if a case of unreasonable and arbitrary statutory procedure were presented, provided it applied equally to the nationals of the government concerned and to foreigners, we should entertain grave doubt as to whether it could be said to operate as a denial of justice so as to lay the foundation for an international claim. . . . The plea that the claimants were ignorant of their rights under the law, and consequently entitled to refunds of duties, regardless of the law, through the award of an international tribunal, cannot be sustained. Importers, whatever their nationality, must be presumed to know and are bound by the customs laws of the countries with which they are dealing.

The records of the tribunal contain the Cadenhead decision of 1914, where the same principle emerges. Elizabeth Cadenhead was

12. Nielsen, *op. cit.,* pp. 347 *seq.*

killed in 1907 by a shot from a sentry's rifle fired after a military prisoner escaping from Fort Brady at Sault Ste Marie, Michigan. A claim for $25,000 as compensation to her relatives was refused. The award runs:

It has not been shown that there was a denial of justice, or that there were any special circumstances or grounds of exception to the generally recognised rule of international law that a foreigner within the United States is subject to its public law, and has no greater rights than nationals of that country.

As between States of approximately equal degrees of civilization and organization, this criterion is normally a sufficient safeguard of justice. It is by no means so acceptable where marked divergence exists in the principles and practice of public order and commercial intercourse. It seems reasonable to demand that the members of the family of nations should offer commensurable security for lawful activities, and be liable for damages resulting from a failure to maintain a common standard. There is as yet no general agreement upon the specific elements of such a standard; but equality of treatment with nationals has not been accepted in lieu thereof as the rule which the tribunal took it to be. There are still fragments of the system of capitulations in the world, and some States still demand special protection for their nationals even where no such arrangement exists by treaty. They assume the right, in other words, of complaining of the general administration of justice within the territory of a fellow member of the international community.

The award in the Hudson Bay Company's Claims,[13] 1869, affords an illustration of circumstances in which such a right of complaint may reasonably be admitted. It is true that in that case the United States had bound themselves by the Oregon Treaty of 1846 to protect the "possessory rights" of the company. Nevertheless, it was the general lawlessness of the population to which the commission referred as ground for the view that the duty of protection was not fulfilled by allowing the claimant access to the ordinary courts,[14] and if general lawlessness imposes special measures where the duty exists

13. See above, pp. 60–63.
14. See Sir John Rose's reasoning, Moore, *op. cit.*, I, 252. The American Commissioner apparently agreed (p. 261).

by treaty, why not also where it exists by the custom of nations? And certainly, though the standard is only vaguely defined, the whole practice of the protection of nationals abroad assumes such a duty. It is still argued in some quarters that, apart from treaty, the whole duty is to afford the same protection to aliens as to nationals. If so, what becomes of the widely accepted principle that the State may be forced to pay a penalty or compensation where injury to an alien results from negligence in prevention or is followed by failure to bring the wrongdoer to justice? Surely it is not a sufficient answer in such cases to point out that nationals suffered similar injury and found no redress.

At the Hague Conference on Codification in 1930, a majority group, including Great Britain, Canada, the other Dominions, and the United States, rejected the criterion of equal treatment in favor of an obligation to maintain a standard "in conformity with the rules of law accepted by the community of nations." A minority, which included most of the Central and South American States, insisted that an alien could expect no better treatment than a national.[15] With such a division on fundamental principle, the hope of progress in matters of detail had to be abandoned.

The equality criterion would really mean that every man enters and resides in a foreign country at his own risk.[16] Its acceptance would undoubtedly eliminate a most fruitful cause of international disputes. But the consequent absence of security in social and commercial relations between peoples might well prove too high a price to pay for such general indulgence, and the disappearance in recent times of all national boundaries to economic and other enterprise intensifies the demand for a uniform international standard of protection. The attainment of such a standard will be another and more progressive way of eliminating friction; but it cannot be expected to operate with automatic perfection, and the right of recourse in cases of alleged failure will have to be preserved. In the definition of the standard lies one of the great problems of "dynamic international law."

15. Parliamentary Report of the Canadian Delegates.

16. Note that the resolution adopted at the 1927 session of the Institute of International Law calls for *at least* the same protection and means of redress for aliens as for nationals. *Annuaire*, 33, 3, p. 331.

Exhaustion of Local Remedies and *Déni de Justice*

The confusion of thought which has reigned in regard to the whole matter of state responsibility for wrongs to aliens is well exemplified by the glaring inconsistency between the statement by the same tribunal (a) that an alien can claim no greater consideration than a national and (b) that ordinary remedies must be exhausted as a condition precedent to the validity of an international claim. For the national has no recourse left when the ordinary remedies are exhausted or refused, whereas everyone seems willing to admit that *déni de justice* gives to the State of an alien the right to claim compensation in his behalf.

It has already been indicated that the criterion of equality is, rightly, in process of abandonment. On the other hand, the principle that available local remedies should be exhausted is sound. It is clearly inexpedient that an international issue should be made of the grievance of a private person who could have obtained adequate redress by recourse to the proper authorities of the country in which he suffered wrong. So much being granted, however, there still remains a wide field of controversy in the question, What constitutes availability and adequacy or, in other words, what exactly is denial of justice?

In the terms of submission signed on July 6, 1911, and appended to the Pecuniary Claims Agreement of the previous year, Great Britain and the United States agreed that:

> The Arbitral Tribunal shall take into account as one of the equities of a claim . . . any failure on the part of the claimants to obtain satisfaction through legal remedies which are open to him or placed at his disposal, but no claim shall be disallowed or rejected by application of the general principle of international law that the legal remedies must be exhausted as a condition precedent to the validity of a claim.

This clause is interesting as one of the relatively rare instances where two great Powers have, as a mere incident to a treaty which does not purport to be lawmaking, stated clearly and officially their acceptance of a rule of law. It is interesting also because it embodies an agreement not to stand on strict legal right for the purpose of the prospective arbitral proceedings. The tribunal is left free to decide how far a claim is to be regarded as vitiated by the neglect of the claimant to take the usual legal steps.

In the *R. T. Roy*[17] the tribunal quite unnecessarily invoked this discretion in dismissing a claim for damages following on the seizure of an American fishing vessel on Lake Huron by a Canadian Fisheries inspector. To support the claim counsel for the United States had to prove that the seizure was effected in American waters, and the tribunal was entirely unsatisfied by his effort to do so. It declared, indeed, that it was "faced by an irreconcilable conflict of untested and untestable statements. The location of the point of seizure is at best a mere guess." Further, "the evidence of damages is inconclusive and unsatisfactory." Why the arbiters should have gone beyond these adequate grounds of dismissal and based their decision on the claimant's failure to take proceedings in Canada against the inspector or against the Government by petition of right, it is difficult to understand. By doing so they gave the American agent some reason for the complaint that they had totally ignored the second part of the treaty provision about exhaustion of legal remedies.

The point had not been raised or argued. If it had been, the tribunal would have been justified in resorting to this *ratio decidendi*, just as it did in the matter of the hay duties, decided on the same day.[18] In the latter award, however, the arbiters again went out of their way, this time to supplement a perfectly satisfactory basis of decision by reference to the unsound principle of equality of treatment.

Another award in which the fact that the claimants had not taken advantage of available ordinary remedies probably weighed against them was that rejecting the claims in respect of the *Argonaut* and *Jonas H. French*. These were two American vessels whose boats and seines were seized for fishing within Canadian waters and condemned in the Prince Edward Island Vice-Admiralty Court. The arbiters found that "the boats and seines being inside the territorial waters, were, from the international law point of view, undoubtedly subject to the municipal law and the jurisdiction of Canada." An early passage, however, runs thus, "It is shown by the documents that the owners, although opportunity was given to them to make the neces-

17. Nielsen, *op. cit.*, pp. 406 *seq.*   18. Above, p. 82.

sary application to the Vice-Admiralty Court, did not exercise their right to have the cases re-opened and to put in their defence before the Court," and the tribunal may well have regarded this as a contemporary confession of the weakness of the case.

Actually, the facts as admitted by the tribunal implied some possible hardship. The boats had seined their fish outside the three-mile limit and drifted in with the tide. Yet the arbiters refused to enter into the question whether, "taking into consideration the good faith of the fishermen and the exact character of their acts, a proper interpretation and application of the Canadian law was made by the Canadian court." To do so, of course, would have been to act as a court of review over the national judiciary, and the tribunal here sheered away from one of the delicate and unsolved problems involved in the vague concept, *déni de justice*. There is much support for the view that a patently erroneous or partial interpretation of the law by the national courts does constitute denial of justice and so engages the international responsibility of the State. But how limit this, how give certainty to such vague terms as "patently" or "outrageously"? Yet, if there is to be maintained a common standard, how escape the conclusion that the international tribunal must in effect, by the very act of inquiring into an alleged failure to observe it, act as a court of review? It would seem that, aside from a theory of sovereignty which has become untenable, there would be no enormity in accepting this as a function of international adjudication.

The award in the case of Robert Brown is of capital importance for its treatment of *déni de justice*. This claim had nothing to do with Canada, but since it was adjudicated by a tribunal whose business was largely Canadian-American, we may be pardoned for a brief summary. Brown was an American citizen who in 1895 applied for licenses in the South African Republic to stake out 1,200 mining claims. The licenses were refused by the competent official and Brown entered suit in the High Court of the Republic. That body found that the refusal had been wrongful and directed that the licenses be issued. President Kruger's Government intervened, prevented the issue of effective licenses and so changed the personnel of the High Court that Brown's subsequent claim for damages was dismissed.

After Great Britain's annexation of the South African Republic, Brown induced the Government of the United States to urge his claim against His Britannic Majesty, and in due course the matter was referred to the Pecuniary Claims Tribunal, which in 1923 found a clear case of denial of justice.

All three branches of the Government conspired to ruin his enterprise. The Executive department issued proclamations for which no warrant could be found in the Constitution and laws of the country. The Volksraad enacted legislation which, on its face, does violence to fundamental principles of justice recognised in every enlightened community. The judiciary, at first recalcitrant, was at length reduced to submission and brought into line with a determined policy of the Executive to reach the desired result regardless of constitutional guarantees and inhibitions.

We are not impressed by the argument founded upon the alleged neglect to exhaust legal remedies by taking out a new summons. . . . In the frequently quoted language of an American Secretary of State:

"A claimant in a foreign State is not required to exhaust justice in such State when there is no justice to exhaust" [Moore's *International Law Digest*, VI, 677].[19]

The tribunal would have awarded damages if the defendant in the proceedings had been the South African Republic. But it was explicit in the opinion that the liability never passed to or was assumed by the British Government.

An instructive feature of the decision is the tribunal's acceptance of the view that the rule requiring exhaustion of local remedies is not literally absolute. When the reorganized High Court dismissed Brown's claim for damages it gave him leave to institute a new action. There was, then, a further step open to him. He was advised, however, by counsel on the spot, that further proceedings would be quite hopeless. The Government had a perfect defense in the law which it had exacted from a subservient legislature and in the oath imposed upon the judges to apply laws and Volksraad resolutions irrespective of their conformity with the Constitution. It would be obviously inequitable for an international tribunal to dismiss a claim

19. Nielsen, *op. cit.*, pp. 198–199. The quotation is from a letter of Mr. Fish, Secretary of State, to Mr. Pile, Minister to Venezuela, May 29, 1873.

on the ground that the claimant had not instituted proceedings which were bound to yield him nothing.

Interference by governments to prevent application of the general law to individual cases in which they have a special interest is one of the few instances of clear denial of justice, and it is far from certain that occasions for invoking this precedent will not present themselves in Canadian-American relations. Legislation, particularly legislation by delegated authority, in periods of political or economic emergency, may well inflict hardships, even in countries with a strong tradition of the rule of law, that can only be remedied by international adjudication.

The American authorities have shown a laudable conservatism in making international issues of private complaints alleging denial of justice. Thus when Capt. George Barker of the American ship *Panther* was kept in jail at Halifax, Nova Scotia, for almost three months, on a charge in which the Government of the United States held that no foreign court had jurisdiction, the Department of State refused to apply to His Britannic Majesty's Government for redress. While Barker was detained, the Supreme Court of Nova Scotia was looking into the competence of the vice-admiralty to entertain the proceedings. Mr. Forsyth, Secretary of State, wrote in these terms:

. . . even if the facts were such as to exclude the judicial cognizance of any foreign tribunal, the case presented would be that of an inferior court assuming an unlawful jurisdiction in a civil suit, in which it was overruled and checked by a superior court, without any appearance of unusual vexation or delay.[20]

In 1887 the American ship *Bridgewater* was detained for 81 days at Shelburne, Nova Scotia, by the collector of customs, and then unconditionally released. The Department of State, on learning that the owner had been informed by the minister of customs, in accordance with an opinion given by the minister of justice, "that he had no redress in the courts against any officer of the Crown," presented the claim to the British Government. On the facts, as stated, here was a flagrant denial of justice. Subsequently, however, it appeared

20. John Bassett Moore, *A Digest of International Law* (Washington, Government Printing Office, 1906), VI, 652–653.

that the owner had in fact begun a suit against the collector in the Supreme Court of Nova Scotia, that this suit was still pending, and that the adverse opinion of the minister of justice had been acknowledged to be based upon an error and withdrawn. The Department thereupon abstained from pressing the claim, in spite of the long detention of the vessel and the discouragements at first put in the claimant's way, "till it should appear that the owner had used his judicial remedies and that justice had been denied."[21]

Relation between the Individual's Claim and His State's Case

Canadian-American litigation arising out of wrongs inflicted on the nationals of the one country in the territory of the other suffers, as does similar litigation elsewhere, from the dual character imposed on all claims by existing ideas of international law. The doctrine which, with certain exceptions,[22] still prevails in practice is that, since the individual is not a person in the law of nations, he cannot sue before an international tribunal. According to this theory the party before such bodies can only be the State and the issue can only be the alleged violation of the right of a State to have its nationals treated in a certain manner by the authorities of other States. Yet the State's case may on the one hand be affected by conduct of the individual subsequent to the wrong and, on the other, be unaffected by conduct on the part of the State which might be expected to endanger its claim. At one moment, in other words, emphasis is thrown on the substantial identity of the State's and the individual's cause of action, at another on their formal separateness.

Some interesting illustrations of this fluctuating identity and dualism are furnished by Canadian-American arbitral decisions under the heading of waiver of claim by the individual, laches on the part of his government, and assessment of damages.

Waiver of claim. Thus, in the *Tattler*,[23] the British-American

21. Moore, *Digest,* VI, 668–669.

22. E.g., the International Joint Commission, between Canada and the United States, where private individuals or concerns press their own applications for permission to obstruct or divert boundary waters (see below, p. 97); and the mixed Arbitral Tribunals set up by the treaties of peace (see, for example, Treaty of Versailles, Articles 299, 300, 304).

23. Nielsen, *op cit.,* pp. 489 *seq.*

Pecuniary Claims Tribunal held that the owners' waiver of all claim against the British Crown, given in consideration of the release of their schooner, deprived the United States of all right of action. The *Tattler* had been arrested by Canadian officials and detained for six days at Liverpool, Nova Scotia, on a charge of violating the treaty of 1818 and the Canadian statute on fishing by foreign vessels. The fine of $500 demanded by the Canadian Government was paid under protest, but no condition or reservation was attached to the waiver of all claim "before any court or Tribunal in respect to said detention . . . or for loss or damage in the premises."

The American agent contended that injury had been done to an American citizen, that such injury was a wrong against the United States and that the United States was not bound by the waiver. If attention had been concentrated here on the infringement of a right of the United States to have its citizens protected against wrongful action on the part of foreign officials, this waiver could hardly have told against the claim. It would have then appeared to be nothing more than an attempted release by one party of a claim belonging to another, and as such void. But the tribunal refused in this instance to distinguish any right in the United States other than that of its national.

Laches. In 1926 the same tribunal awarded to the Cayuga Indians resident in Canada $100,000 as compensation for the refusal of the State of New York to pay them a share of the annuity promised to the Cayuga Nation by treaties of 1789, 1790, and 1795.[24] No payment had been made since 1810, and the Canadian Cayugas had since 1814 repeatedly urged the British Government to take the matter up with the United States. Nevertheless, it was not until 1899 that the British Minister at Washington had brought the case to the attention of the State Department and when the matter finally came to arbitration, the American agent argued that the whole claim should be held barred by this laches on the part of Great Britain. The tribunal admitted the laches of Great Britain but held that

dependent Indians, not free to act except through the appointed agencies of a sovereign which has a complete and exclusive protectorate

24. Nielsen, *op. cit.*, pp. 203–331.

over them, are not to lose their just claims through the laches of that sovereign. . . .

This award commends itself by its conformity with principles of substantial equity. Technically, however, it is marred by confusion between the Indians and the real party before the tribunal, namely the Crown of Great Britain, and on this point Mr. Nielsen's sharp criticism is justified.[25] The confusion is the more remarkable in that the arbiters had declared in deciding a preliminary question, "This Tribunal is constituted by virtue of a treaty between the United States and Great Britain and can recognize no other parties to the controversies before it."[26] This defect is, however, anything but unique. It is safe to predict that it will be frequently repeated so long as the artificial construction, which makes the State the party, while finding the equities of each case in the conduct of the individuals concerned in the original wrong, is not replaced by permission to the private person to present his own claim.

Assessment of damages. Nowhere does the dualism in the treatment of the claimant party make itself more apparent than at the point of assessing damages. Where a state has failed to take precautions necessary to prevent acts which in the particular circumstances it would reasonably be expected to guard against, it may with justice be called upon to make full compensation for ensuing damage, and the injury suffered by the victim of such acts is a good measure. Here the plaintiff State may be regarded, without undue violence to logic, as suffering the same degree of damage as its national. The same may be said of positive wrongs done by the agents of a State. But where the sole delinquency of the State is failure to apprehend and punish a wrongdoer, it is by definition not responsible for the wrongful act itself and the damages suffered by the victim in consequence of that act should accordingly not be brought into account. Logically, the measure for any award in damages in such cases should be the loss suffered by the State (or, as above, by its national, since this measure of identification is permissible) in consequence solely of the non-punishment of the culprit. But if this measure were generally adopted, there would frequently be no award in damages at all, and any amount ordered to be paid would have to be looked upon as frankly penal.

25. *Op. cit.*, at pp. 271–273.   26. *Ibid.*, p. 272.

"Arbitral tribunals," says Professor Eagleton,[27] "have rarely been willing to award penalties, in the form of money payment beyond the damages actually occasioned, perhaps because of the absence of agreement in the treaty under which they have worked." A more general reason has been the reluctance of jurists to admit that the wrongful acts of sovereign States might be penalized by international law in precisely the same manner as wrongful acts of a private person are penalized by municipal law. This objection is losing ground, however, and as Professor Eagleton himself later observes, "It can no longer be argued that the sovereign state is above the law; and there seems to be no reason why it should not be penalised for its misconduct under proper rules and restrictions."[28]

What has happened in the past is that the State defendant has either been mulcted in the amount of damage resulting from an act for the commission of which it was not held liable, or, as in the famous Janes case between the United States and Mexico, been ordered to pay an exaggerated or fictitious estimate of the damage resulting to the individual from failure to prosecute. The first mode of procedure is both illogical and inequitable, the second amounts to penal sentence under disguise.[29]

The schooner *I'm Alone*, built and registered in Nova Scotia, was sunk on March 22, 1929, by a United States Coast Guard vessel at a point on the high sea more than two hundred miles from the American coast. She had admittedly been engaged in carrying liquor for transshipment at convenient points off the coast to American vessels which smuggled the cargo into the United States. The crew of the *I'm Alone* were plunged by the sinking of their craft into a rough sea and one member drowned. The master and surviving members were taken on board by two American Coast Guard vessels, placed in irons and conveyed to New Orleans where they were kept in custody for forty-eight hours before being released on bail. The charges against them were subsequently dropped.

27. Clyde Eagleton, *The Responsibility of States in International Law* (New York, 1928), p. 190.

28. *Ibid.*, p. 191.

29. For an excellent study of the inconsistencies of arbitral procedure in this matter, illustrated by an analysis of the Janes and other cases, see Frederick Sherwood Dunn, *The Protection of Nationals* (Baltimore, 1932), pp. 172 *seq.*

Under the terms of the liquor treaty of 1924, the claim entered by Canada in consequence of these facts was referred to a commission consisting of the Chief Justice of the Supreme Court of Canada and a judge of the Supreme Court of the United States. In their final report they found that the sinking of the *I'm Alone* was unjustified and recommended payment to Canada under two distinct heads. The first recommendation was that the United States should formally acknowledge the illegality of the sinking, apologize to His Majesty's Canadian Government, and "as a material amend in respect of the wrong" should pay $25,000 to that Government; the second was that the United States should pay a total sum of $25,666.50 to the Canadian Government for the benefit of the captain and crew or their legal representatives as compensation for the damage which they had suffered.

The second part of this report is of the usual type. The United States had been found liable for the wrongful act of its officials, and was recommended to pay an amount covering the individual damages proved to the satisfaction of the commission. The commission had rejected—and this is a point of some interest—all claim by the owner to compensation for the loss of the ship and cargo. The legal owner was a company incorporated in Nova Scotia, but it was found that the *I'm Alone* was "*de facto* owned, controlled, and at the critical times, managed . . . by a group of persons acting in concert who were entirely, or nearly so, citizens of the United States." These persons were engaged in operations contrary to the law of their country, and the commissioners apparently agreed that it would have been inequitable to exact reparation from that country for losses inflicted in the course of law enforcement on the conspirators. The position of the captain and crew was different, since they were held to have been no party to the "illegal conspiracy to smuggle liquor into the United States and sell the same there." The significant thing is that the commission held itself competent to look behind the mask of Nova Scotia incorporation and determine this part of their recommendation by the nationality of the individuals substantially interested.

The first part of the report, on the other hand, is quite extraordinary. Not only does it constitute a penal award against a sovereign State, which, as Professor Eagleton has observed, is a rare thing; but this award was arrived at without apparent authority either in the treaty of 1924 or in the issue as presented by the States parties to the dispute. It is true that the commission was not in name arbitral and that its conclusions were nominally recommendations rather than an arbitral award. But that they have the same force as an arbitral award is clear from the undertaking in Article 4 of the treaty that "effect shall be given to the recommendations contained in any such joint report." The commission might therefore have been expected to act with careful respect for the limits marked out in the instrument providing for its establishment. That instrument, the liquor treaty of 1924, provided merely that "any claim by a British vessel for compensation on the ground that it has suffered loss or injury through the improper or unreasonable exercise of the rights conferred by article 2 . . ." should be referred to two persons, one nominated by each of the high contracting parties. There is no mention whatever of any claim by the country itself. Furthermore, nothing in the published claim presented by the Canadian Government even suggests a demand for compensation in respect of the wrong to Canada.

Professor Hyde has the following to say on this subject:

It should also be observed that the claim of that [the Canadian] Government embraced an item of expenses incurred in repatriating the crew, amounting to $6,109.41, and embracing "legal expenses" amounting to $27,701.02, the total item being $33,810.43. The $25,000 recommended for payment to the Canadian Government, apart from the reasons suggested by the Commissioners, constituted partial compensation for expenses incurred by it in the prosecution of its case against the United States. For that reason, the recommendation of the Commissioners that this sum be paid to the Canadian Government may be deemed to lack importance as a precedent indicative of the propriety of the imposition by an arbitral tribunal or by a joint commission of penal damages against a respondent State in satisfaction of an essentially public claim.[30]

But the Canadian Government made no claim whatever in its own behalf, so far at least as the record shows, in respect of legal expenses and repatriation of the crew or of anything else. These items appear solely as part of the claim advanced in behalf of the Eugene

30. *A.J.I.L.*, April, 1935, p. 300.

Creaser Shipping Company, Ltd., the whole of which was rejected by the commissioners.

It is difficult, moreover, to suppose that two such eminent jurists would have chosen what would amount to a ruse for bringing in under a totally foreign head compensation refused in its proper place. The only legitimate conclusion is that they intended the $25,000 to be a definitely penal amend, and, in spite of Professor Hyde's observations, the report is most likely to figure as a precedent. If it should then be attacked as exceeding the terms of reference to the commission, some answer may be found in that section of the American answering brief cited, with much greater cogency, in an earlier part of Professor Hyde's note, and running as follows:

. . . if the Commissioners interpret their function as that of authoritative advisers to the two Governments, they may properly make to either Government any recommendation upon which they can agree with respect either to the further pressing of the claim or to any other phase of the controversy.

Here indeed was something which the commissioners could interpret as an indefinite extension of their competence.

Any perusal of the records of arbitration reveals that international law on the subject of damages and penalties is in a thoroughly unsatisfactory state. I am suggesting that this is due to a failure to draw a clear distinction between the interest of the State and the interest of its national. These interests may be admitted to coincide at least partially where damage to the national results from the act or neglect of an official of the foreign government. Even here, however, the State plaintiff may have an interest, over and above that of the individual national, in the preservation of an international standard violated by the said act or omission, or in the protection of its own rightful sphere of competence against foreign encroachment.

Much, it seems, would be gained by careful definition in *compromis* or schedule of claims of the exact issue between the States parties. Is the State plaintiff suing to obtain compensation to be paid eventually, if not directly, to the injured national, or is it suing for redress in respect of its own rights as a State? This is the minimum of change which should be made in arbitral practice. A more effective reform would be to allow, in the first class of claims, the individual to plead his own case before the arbitral tribunal. This would strip away all the existing artificiality involved in the adoption by the State as its own of a claim which is essentially personal to the injured individual. That it would imply recognition of the individual as a subject of international law is a formal objection which only the most conservative jurists will continue to urge. The contemporary tendency to regard international law as a system imposing duties rather than conferring or confirming state rights will facilitate such a development. Given this emphasis on duty, what substantial objection can there be to admitting that the State may be under a direct obligation to an alien? Any danger of a flooding of international courts by trifling claims could be avoided by the requirement of a preliminary leave to be issued by the claimant's government. If that government felt that, in addition to the wrong to its national, a wrong had also been inflicted on the State which it represents, it might be allowed to join as a party or to institute separate proceedings. The excellent work of the International Joint Commission between the United States and Canada, and the general satisfaction felt in both countries over the results which it has achieved, furnish cogent evidence that the procedure here recommended is both efficient and acceptable.[31]

INTERNATIONAL SERVITUDES

Two neighboring countries so long at peace as the United States and Canada would seem to offer ideal circumstances for the growth of international servitudes. The increasing sense of interdependence between all nations and of common interest between these two in particular calls for the recognition in the international sphere of an institution which has proven its economic and social usefulness in municipal law. And in fact the Republic and Dominion have from time to time adopted arrangements which present the external characteristics of servitude. This has occurred in regard to fisheries, and

31. Applications from private persons for approval of the use, obstruction, or diversion of boundary waters go first to the applicant's government and are then, if approved by the government, forwarded to the commission. The applicant, however, appears as a party in the subsequent proceedings. See *Rules of Procedure of the International Joint Commission* (Washington, 1913), S. 6, ss.b.

in regard to land and water communications. Yet we have not aided theoretically in a development which is greatly to be desired,[32] for when it has come to the test both sides have shrunk from acknowledging that these arrangements possess all the legal nature of servitude. One factor which has weighed heavily against such an acknowledgment has been the clash between servitude and the traditional concept of sovereignty, a clash probably sharpened by the formal antithesis of the terms themselves.

FISHERIES

We have already discussed the provisions of the treaty of 1818[33] granting to the inhabitants of the United States the liberty in perpetuity to fish in certain of the Atlantic coastal waters of Newfoundland and Canada, and the long series of disputes, culminating in the North Atlantic Fisheries Arbitration of 1909, to which these provisions gave rise. One of the contentions advanced in support of the American case in the arbitration last named was that the liberty to fish constituted a servitude which limited the legislative power of Newfoundland and Canada in treaty waters.

The right or liberty—and all the ingenious argument of counsel for Great Britain fails to establish a substantial difference in this context between liberty and right—granted to the inhabitants of one country to take fish in the territory of another is clearly of the same nature as certain Roman law servitudes, such as the right to draw water, dig sand, or make lime, and as the English *profits à prendre*. The Hague tribunal in its elaborate examination of this point did not reject all notion of servitude in international law: it merely refused to recognize the existence of the institution otherwise than on the express evidence of an international contract. As express evidence, it would apparently have demanded the actual use of the

32. Publicists are by no means agreed on the question whether the law of nations admits or should admit servitudes. See for example, McNair in *British Year Book of International Law* (1925), pp. 111 *seq.* In the "Wimbledon" the Permanent Court of International Justice described this question as "one of a very controversial nature," which indicates clearly enough that there is as yet no settled law on the matter. *Permanent Court of International Justice,* Series A, No. 1, p. 24.

33. Above, pp. 24–41.

term. Its statement[34] that "a servitude in international law predicates an express grant of a sovereign right—whereas by the treaty of 1818 one State grants a liberty to fish, which is not a sovereign right, but a purely economic right" (note the identification of liberty and right) carries no conviction, first, because the distinction between sovereign and economic rights is at best a vague and doubtful one,[35] and, second, because the chief *raison d'être* of servitude is precisely its economic utility. The real burden of the tribunal's objection to interpreting the right in question as a servitude lay in what we may now hope to be a somewhat obsolete doctrine of sovereignty and the incompatibility of a relation of *praedium dominans* and *praedium serviens* with the tenets of that doctrine. The arbiters were on sounder ground when they added that "even if these liberties of fishery constituted an international servitude" that construction would not render the servient State incompetent to enact reasonable regulations "for the purpose of securing and preserving the fishery and its exercise for the common benefit." British counsel, in other words, need not have denied the existence of servitude to maintain the right of regulation.

This decision, though, as already observed, the arbiters did not come out flatly against the institution in dispute, displayed something approaching hostility to it, and has constituted an obstacle to progress in the matter. For the discussion occurs in the very forefront of the tribunal's award and is constantly cited by jurists concerned with international arrangements of this type.

An argument often advanced against the admission of servitude into international law is that these rights cannot and should not be made binding upon a successor in title to the servient territory. There would, however, be no greater difficulty in this than in securing observance of any other duty. Once the right has been granted in due form and in perpetuity, there is no reason why it should not be regarded as running with the land. A successor, whether by cession or by conquest, would then take the territory with its burdens, the servient State being incapable of ceding or yielding any fuller rights than it itself had.

34. *North Atlantic Coast Fisheries Arbitration*, I, 76.
35. Is it not a sovereign right, if anything is, for the State to demand that its nationals be given the privileges promised them in a treaty?

As to the effect of war upon the exercise of such rights, they might well be regarded as merely in suspense while conditions of fact made their use substantially inconvenient. On the declaration of peace, they would automatically spring into activity again. This, it is submitted, would be the proper way to treat perpetual rights of passage across territorial land or water and any other permanent uses of the resources of a foreign State.

Land and Water Communications

Unfortunately this view has not found favor. When the Jay Treaty of 1794 laid down in its third article that

it shall at all times be free to His Majesty's subjects, and to the citizens of the United States . . . freely to pass and repass by land or inland navigation, into the respective territories and countries of the two parties . . . and to navigate all the lakes, rivers and waters thereof, and freely to carry on trade and commerce with each other,

it set up something that had all the appearance of a permanent right of passage in the nature of a mutual servitude. The expression "at all times" coupled with the description, in a later part of the treaty, of Articles 1 to 10 as permanent, and read in the knowledge of the needs which the treaty was designed to meet, seems to demonstrate the intention to make this a perpetual freedom. The United States Circuit Court of Appeals accepted this interpretation in 1928 and held that this Article was not abrogated by the War of 1812.[36] The Supreme Court[37] took the opposite view, declared that the Article had not been in effect since 1812, and maintained the validity of a regulation issued by the Department of Labor in 1927 to prevent British subjects not born in Canada from crossing over daily from Windsor to work in Detroit. Thus was a useful arrangement of good neighborhood defeated by unnecessary legal conservatism, for it is submitted that the classification of these arrangements as real covenants running with the land would preserve them against destruction by war.

The judicial decision of the Supreme Court had been long preceded by a political one in the same sense by the British Government.

36. *United States* v. *Karnuth,* 24 *Federal Reporter,* 2d series, 649 *seq.*
37. *U.S. Supreme Court Reports,* October Term, 1928, pp. 677 *seq.*

After the War of 1812 the British authorities considered themselves free, notwithstanding the right of navigation and commerce granted by the Jay Treaty of 1794, to restrict at will the movement of American trade in those portions of the St. Lawrence River which were wholly Canadian. Restrictions actually imposed induced the inhabitants of Franklin County in the State of New York to petition Congress to obtain for them the right of exporting their lumber and other products down river to the Atlantic. The matter was taken up by the Department of State which, through its Ministers in London, urged a natural right of navigation in favor of upper riparian communities. Such a right was never admitted by Great Britain to exist by the general law of nations, and it was only in consideration of a *quid pro quo* that the desired freedom was granted temporarily by the Reciprocity Treaty of 1854 and permanently by the Washington Treaty of 1871. Article 25 of the latter instrument provides that the navigation of the St. Lawrence

shall forever remain free and open for the purpose of commerce to the citizens of the United States, subject to any laws and regulations of Great Britain or the Dominion of Canada, not inconsistent with such privilege of free navigation,

and accords a corresponding privilege to British subjects on the rivers Yukon, Porcupine, and Stikine.

It is submitted that these mutual concessions are intended to be perpetual and irrevocable and that all the reasons which justify the running of covenants with the land in municipal law exist here for analogous treatment. Happily the possibility of war between the parties is a more than ordinarily remote one, but theory should admit at most the suspension of the right of navigation in such an eventuality.

ACQUISITIVE PRESCRIPTION

The Privy Council held in *Direct United States Cable Co.* v. *Anglo-American Telegraph Co.*[38] that Conception Bay in Newfoundland had become by prescription part of the territory of Great Britain. This was an appeal from an order of the Supreme Court of Newfoundland restraining the appellant company from laying a cable

38. *Law Reports,* 1877, 2 Appeal Cases at p. 421.

anywhere within the jurisdiction of the colony in violation of exclusive rights granted by the legislature to the respondents; and the
Judicial Committee sustained the order. The finding that title had
accrued by prescription was based principally upon two assertions
of sovereignty and the absence of protest by any nation against
them. The assertions occurred in the Fisheries Treaty of 1818, by
which it was agreed that American fishermen should not be permitted to enter certain bays in Newfoundland, including Conception
Bay, except for the purposes of shelter, repairing damages, purchasing wood, and obtaining water; and in an Act of Parliament of
1819, which imposed a penalty of £200 upon any alien who dis-
obeyed an official order to depart from such bays.

This decision figured prominently in the British case in the North
Atlantic Fisheries Arbitration of 1910. The Americans were then
contending that the only bays "of His Britannic Majesty's Dominions in America" from which their fishermen were excluded by this
clause in the treaty of 1818 were those under British sovereignty,
and that no bay over six miles in width was territorial. The British
Government refused to accept either of these propositions, arguing
that the word "bays" in the treaty was used merely in the geographical sense, and that many bays of much greater width than
six miles were generally conceded to be part of the national territory
not only in the British Empire and the United States, but in other
countries as well. On both points Great Britain was sustained by the
tribunal, and the award clearly admits the possibility of acquiring
title to bays far exceeding the limits applying in the marginal belt
of sea.

But is acquisition by prescription the correct legal description of
what occurs in these cases? There are two possible ways of regarding
the sea. It is either *res nullius*, or it is the public property of the
international community, and juristic treatment of its appropriation has for centuries fluctuated between these two views. If the first
view is taken, then the sole prerequisite of title is effective control,
and the mode of acquisition is not prescription but occupation. The
possession which results in prescription is essentially *adverse* possession, and where the object is *res nullius* there is by definition no
one against whom the holding can be adverse. Between the two modes
there is this important practical difference, that whereas prescrip-

tion in international law requires the passage of a considerable though not yet defined time, effective occupation gives immediate ownership. On the other hand, if the sea is to be regarded as common to all men, public property of the *civitas maxima*, then it is *extra commercium* and its appropriation by individual States is legally impossible.

Now the essential element in the reasoning which has gradually led to the recognition of sovereignty in a marginal belt of at least three miles is the possibility of effective control within that limit. That thought is at the bottom of Bynkershoek's famous dictum, *Terrae potestas finitur ubi finitur armorum vis*, which is accepted as the starting point of the modern law on the subject. Behind it is the assumption that the sea is susceptible of reduction to ownership, is, in other words, *res nullius* rather than *res publica*. But in the discussion of bays, prominence is given to the consideration that they lie outside the lines of commerce as justifying their appropriation by the States whose territory encloses them. This reasoning is valid only if the open sea is regarded as a sort of public domain, while bays, on the other hand, because they are off the common highway and not of immediate importance to the general welfare, are classified as areas open to *occupatio*.

The American case for exclusive control of the sealing industry in the Behring Sea oscillated from prescription, through estoppel by acquiescence, to the appropriation by *occupatio* of animals *ferae naturae*. For prescription or estoppel the historical evidence was fatal, since it demonstrated, on the part of Great Britain, active opposition to, rather than acquiescence in, the Russian claims upon which the United States based their argument. Here also it should have been realized that, as the seals were obviously *res nullius*, there could in any case be no question of acquisition by prescription. As for *occupatio*, nothing approaching effective possession of the seal herds could be established; and we have already seen[39] how the tribunal rejected the analogy between the annual breeding visit to the Pribilof Islands and the *animus revertendi* which Roman law recognized as an element in the title to doves and tamed deer.

When the Alaskan boundary was in course of arbitration, British counsel, disregarding the Privy Council's decision in *Direct United*

39. Above, p. 80.

States Cable Co. v. *Anglo-American Telegraph Co.*, denied the existence of any rule of prescription in international law, and the denial seems to have found favor with Lord Alverstone, President, and Mr. Aylesworth, one of the Canadian members of the tribunal.[40] The purpose of this contention was to defeat any attempt on the part of the United States to make the point that it had acquired sovereignty in the land around the inlets by a prescription consisting in the actual holding, policing, and administering of that land, first by Russia and then by the United States, without any protest from Great Britain, for more than seventy years after the Anglo-Russian boundary treaty of 1825. American counsel, however, argued not from prescription, but from the safer ground that Great Britain's acquiescence was a contemporary and long-continued admission that it was the intention of the treaty of 1825 to run the boundary so as to include the heads of the inlets in Russian territory. They employed unprotested possession, in other words, as evidence of the correctness of their interpretation of the treaty, not as creating title not previously owned. The case does little, then, either to establish or disprove the rule of prescription in the law of nations.

Of all the issues dealt with in these three great arbitrations the one which came nearest to the field of operation of prescription properly so called was this question of sovereignty at the heads of the Alaskan inlets. Even there, however, to invoke prescription in favor of Russia and, after her, of the United States, would have been to admit a previously existing title in Great Britain, for, as pointed out above, one does not prescribe a *res nullius*. American counsel, very wisely in view of the hostility to the doctrine of prescription displayed by Lord Alverstone and Mr. Aylesworth, expressly disclaimed the intention of resting their case on this ground. In the fur-seals arbitration ten years earlier, Lord Hannen had incidentally declared against prescription as a part of international law. The arbiters in the North Atlantic Fisheries dispute, on the other hand, accepted it in 1910 without question, but in a matter where it was not strictly relevant and in any event was not necessary to their decision.

What the disputes cited do show very clearly is the need of a sharp distinction between the field of prescription and that of *occu-*

40. *Alaskan Boundary Tribunal,* VI, 344–346.

patio. There appears to be a growing acceptance of prescription as a necessary institution in the law of nations, but it will be a grave misfortune if this addition to our system is vitiated by precedents invoking it in circumstances to which it is not germane.

THE EFFECT OF WAR UPON TREATIES

JURISTIC opinion and diplomatic practice in regard to the effect of war upon treaties have shown equal divergence. Text writers and the agents of States alike have declared that all treaties are automatically canceled on the outbreak of war; but there has long been a great weight of authority against this proposition. The more general practice and opinion admit the possibility of survival, but there is again difference as to the conditions upon which survival depends. As recently as 1912 the Institute of International Law,[41] in a resolution which begins by stating a general rule against the termination of treaties, conventions, and agreements, whatever their title or object, admits among other exceptions that the commencement of hostilities always puts an end to a treaty whose application or interpretation has been the direct cause of war. It is doubtful, however, whether present opinion would support either this statement of the general rule or the specified exception to it.

Prevalent doctrine and practice seem rather to support a general rule of abrogation by war when the belligerents are the sole parties to the treaty, but to admit, by way of exception, the continuance of certain types of arrangement.[42] The criterion determining termination or survival is not what caused the war, but exclusively the nature of the arrangement. This is not to deny that a victorious belligerent in a war arising out of the application or interpretation of an agreement may impose a new treaty as a condition of peace. The sole point is that the cause of hostilities has no bearing on the question as to what treaties are immediately and automatically brought to an end by the cessation of peace.

If this be true, it means that present opinion is rallying around the classic authority of two much-cited decisions. The first is that of the Supreme Court of the United States in *The Society for the*

41. *Annuaire, 25,* p. 648.
42. Cf. Pitt Cobbett, *Leading Cases on International Law* (4th ed. London, 1924), II, 48.

Propagation of the Gospel v. *New Haven*, 1823, where the Court declared that

> treaties stipulating for permanent rights, and general arrangements, and professing to aim at perpetuity, and to deal with the case of war as well as of peace, do not cease on the occurrence of war, but are, at most, only suspended while it lasts; and unless they are waived by the parties, or new and repugnant stipulations are made, they revive in their operation at the return of peace.[43]

The second case is *Sutton* v. *Sutton*,[44] decided by the English Court of Chancery in 1830. The decision here, like that of the United States Supreme Court just cited, upheld Article IX of the Jay Treaty (which guaranteed the estates of British subjects in American territory and of American citizens in British territory) as unaffected by the War of 1812. Leach, M.R., rested his judgment upon what he believed to be the intention of the contracting parties that "the operation of the treaty should be permanent, and not depend upon the continuance of a state of peace."

The same considerations should have preserved the third article of the Jay Treaty, in which mutual rights of passage across the boundary and of navigation in inland waters were granted to the subjects of the contracting Powers. Yet as we have seen in the discussion of servitudes,[45] British governments of the early nineteenth century treated this article as abrogated by the War of 1812, and to their treatment the Supreme Court in 1929 added its judicial decision to the same effect. The *ratio decidendi* in the Supreme Court's pronouncement is, however, interesting for our present purpose. Upon the general question, Mr. Justice Sutherland, who delivered the opinion, has this to say:

> The doctrine sometimes asserted, especially by the older writers, that war *ipso facto* annuls treaties of every kind between the warring nations, is repudiated by the great weight of modern authority; and the view now commonly accepted is that "whether the stipulations of a treaty are annulled by war depends upon their intrinsic character."
> 5 Moore, *International Law Dig.*, §779, p. 383.[46]

43. 8 *Wheaton*, 494–495.   44. 1 *Russell and Mylne*, 663.
45. Above, pp. 100–101.
46. *U.S. Supreme Court Reports*, October Term, 1928, p. 680. Cf. 1 *N.A.C.F.A.*, Award 1, p. 75, "International law in its modern development

Unfortunately, this admirable conclusion was held not to save the stipulation in question, for Article III was declared, by a dubious process of interpretation, not to confer a vested and perpetual right.

As in regard to the navigation clause of the Jay Treaty, so in regard to the fisheries provisions of the treaty of peace of 1783, Great Britain took the view that these were terminated by the outbreak of hostilities in 1812. When the Treaty of Ghent was being negotiated in 1814, the British plenipotentiaries stated that

the British Government did not intend to grant to the United States gratuitously the privileges formerly granted by treaty to them of fishing within the limits of the British Sovereignty and of using the shores of the British territories for purposes connected with the fisheries.[47]

The United States firmly maintained that these privileges were part of the conditions upon which "the two parts of one empire had mutually agreed, thenceforth, to constitute two distinct and separate nations," and were no more forfeited by war than "any other of the rights of our national independence."[48] An attempt was made to combine a recognition of the continuance of the fishing liberties with a new definition of the boundary west of the Lake of the Woods and an acknowledgment of the right of British subjects to navigate the Mississippi, but disagreement both as to the form and the substance of the proposed article caused all mention of fisheries and the Mississippi to be omitted. It was not until 1818, after four years of negotiation punctuated by the seizure of American vessels, that the position was regulated by a new treaty in which the United States obtained some, but by no means all, of the rights previously enjoyed.

It may be of great immediate advantage for a State in a strong position to use the pretext of an intervening war for the purpose of canceling or limiting rights granted, even with a clearly permanent intention, by previous treaty. The practice does, however, militate unnecessarily against stability in international arrangements of an economic order, and it will probably be more profitable all round if the new doctrine of temporary suspension, only, in such cases, is

recognises that a great number of treaty obligations are not annulled by war, but at most suspended by it."

47. See 1 *N.A.C.F.A.*, Case of the United States, p. 14.
48. *Ibid.*, p. 16.

established beyond question. There is of course always the possibility of negotiating fresh agreements at the conclusion of peace, but the history of the fisheries between 1814 and 1818 shows how long normal relations may have to wait for resumption and how full of dangerous incident the interim may be. The natural tendency of interested parties will be to resume at once, upon the establishment of peace, activities permitted by the treaty, and the shock of arrest and confiscation puts a heavy strain upon international good will.

NATURAL LAW AND THE LAW OF NATIONS

THE argument and decision of Canadian-American disputes have afforded occasion for some discussion of the nature and sources of international law and the general principles by which an arbiter must be governed. It is not surprising to find that counsel have relied heavily upon the law of nature in support of their clients' claims, or even that, in the earlier part of the nineteenth century, American Secretaries of State should have larded their protests against alleged arbitrary acts on the part of British officials with references to the same vague but abundant authority. Mr. John Quincy Adams in 1823 rested the case for free navigation of the St. Lawrence upon "general principles of the law of nature"; while Mr. Clay, three years later, maintained that

from the very nature of such a river, it must, in respect of its navigable uses, be considered as common to all the nations who inhabit its banks, as a free gift flowing from the bounty of Heaven, intended for all whose lots are cast upon its borders.[49]

Those were the days of revolutionary constitutions redolent of natural rights, but it was perhaps also to be expected that an unreclaimed and conservative Great Britain would turn a deaf ear to the appeal. And in fact Whitehall exacted its *quid pro quo*.

What is more striking is that, as the century turned positivist, not merely counsel and officials, but arbiters as well, should have continued to invoke natural law. The prolonged and involved negotiations over the seizure of Canadian vessels in Behring Sea, the arguments by which the United States endeavored to establish a right of ownership in the fur seals, and, finally, the dissenting opinions of

49. Moore, *Digest,* I, 631–633.

the American members of the tribunal, bring in this *jus naturale* as the *ratio non scripta* behind all law. Says Mr. Justice Harlan:

One of the recognised sources of the law of nations are the principles of natural reason and justice applicable to the relations and intercourse of independent political societies. Those principles may be said to have their origin in the Law of Nature. . . . Certainly, this Tribunal of Arbitration must regard the rules of international morality and justice . . . as an integral part of the law of nations by which the matters submitted to it are to be determined. . . . Nations, no more than individuals, may disregard those rules, for upon their observance depends the existence of organised society and the security of government among civilised peoples.[50]

Mr. Justice Harlan was speaking in 1893. Since that time, the style, rather than the substance of his reasoning, has become even more old-fashioned. International tribunals of today are shy of the term "natural law," though, by an erroneous interpretation, certain new movements in juristic thought are currently represented as reviving the naturalist school. It is nevertheless true that the very same reasoning for which authority was sought in the law of nature is still employed under a different name. When no precise rule can be proved, or when the strict application of an admitted rule would work what is felt to be gross hardship, arbitral tribunals have recourse, unless prohibited from so doing by their terms of reference, to "general principles of equity."

Thus, in 1926, when the British-American Pecuniary Claims Tribunal was considering the demand of the Canadian Cayuga Indians for a share in certain annuities paid by the State of New York, a careful study of modern arbitral practice led to the conclusion

that something more than the strict law must be used in the grounds of decision of arbitral tribunals in certain cases; that there are cases in which—like the courts of the land—these tribunals must find the grounds of decision, must find the right and the law, in general considerations of justice, equity, and right dealing guided by legal analogies and by the spirit and received principles of international law.

This statement which, as the tribunal suggested, is as true of the judicial process formally so called as it is of arbitration, merely pre-

50. *Fur Seal Arbitration*, Vol. I, Opinion of Mr. Justice Harlan, p. 134.

sents a commonplace of civilized legal systems. Everywhere *lacunae* in the details of law are filled in, and rough places are smoothed out, by reference to general ideas, prevalent at the time in the legal profession, of what is right and fair. These ideas have little connection with "nature"; they are the product of civilization itself, determined by the lawyer's estimate of social values.

CHAPTER VII

THE EXISTING MACHINERY OF SETTLEMENT AND ITS DEFECTS

THE long-standing peace between the United States and Canada is a commonplace which the statesmen of North America are not likely to allow the rest of the world to forget. Their reminders are usually accompanied by vague references to the International Joint Commission as though that admirable body were the sole or principal agency by which good relations are preserved. As a matter of fact the commission is of recent foundation and, as will be shown, of quite limited scope; and it may be said in general that, if peace had had to depend upon perfection in the machinery of settlement between the Republic and Dominion, it could scarcely have lasted through its famous century and a quarter.

Actually of course there is a deep-seated sympathy between the two peoples, a sympathy not to be concealed from a discerning observer by those violent strictures on persons and things American which, in Canada at least, express the sharp but superficial annoyances that inevitably arise from time to time out of crowded intercourse with a powerful and occasionally absent-minded neighbor. It is that sympathy, rather than any nicely adjusted arbitral organization, which is mainly responsible for the settlement of our differences without recourse to arms. For our system of treaties, tribunals, and commissions, far from showing the way to a war-scarred Europe, lags behind the arbitral arrangements now in force between many of the States of the Old World.

It is my purpose to examine now all the special agencies set up for the peaceable handling of conflicts of interest between Canada and the United States, with a view to making clear the limits of their competence and the gaps through which disputes of many kinds have fallen or may fall. This examination will be followed by some suggestions as to how the said *lacunae* might be filled.

The reader will not forget that, in addition to these special agencies, there are always the permanent diplomatic missions maintained by the United States at Ottawa and by Canada at Washington. Long before the establishment of a distinct Canadian Legation in the American capital and the sending of an American minister plenipotentiary to Ottawa, many claims and conflicts were disposed of by negotiation between the Canadian Government and the Department of State through the intermediary of the British Minister accredited to the President. The more direct and specialized channel of communications inaugurated in 1927 should in an increasing measure remove the causes of conflict or at any rate dispose of complaints before they reach the point where arbitration becomes necessary. The resulting new diplomatic history will doubtless be recorded from time to time by future students. Our concern here is, however, with the organs specifically dedicated to adjudication, arbitration, or conciliation, and, however expert our diplomatic service may prove, it is safe to assume that there will always be occasion for such organs. That being so, simple logic demands that they should be made as nearly perfect as possible.

GENERAL ARBITRATION TREATIES

Hague Convention, 1899

Great Britain and the United States were both parties to the Hague Convention of 1899 on the Pacific Settlement of International Disputes.[1] That convention bound them "to use their best efforts to insure the pacific settlement of international differences";[2] and "in case of serious disagreement or conflict, before an appeal to arms, . . . to have recourse, as far as circumstances allow, to the good offices or mediation of one or more friendly Powers."[3] It went on to define the object of arbitration, and to lay down the rule that an agreement to submit to arbitration "implies the engagement to submit loyally to the Award."[4] Thirty-eight articles are then devoted to the organization and procedure of a permanent court of arbitration. What was created was not, however, a court in the ordinary sense, but merely a panel of judges of whom four are appointed by each of the high contracting parties. Nor did the convention impose any obligation to arbitrate, recourse to the Court being

1. For the text, see *Treaties and Agreements,* pp. 107 *seq.*
2. Article 1.   3. Article 2.
4. Article 18.

entirely optional and dependent, in every case, upon a special act (*compromis*) signed by the parties to the dispute and defining the subject of the difference and the extent of the arbitrators' powers. The signatories of the Hague convention were, moreover, left free, if they desired to arbitrate any question, to employ the machinery there provided or any other. If, however, they decide to have recourse to the so-called Permanent Court of Arbitration, they must constitute the specific tribunal to deal with their difference from the general list of members of the Court. Article 24 lays down the procedure to be followed if they cannot reach direct agreement in the selection from this list.

Canada's independent participation in agreements of this sort is a product of postwar development; and the Dominion has not, since achieving its present status in international affairs, signified its adherence to the convention of 1899, nor has it directly elected judges to the panel.[5] Its inclusion in the international personality of Great Britain at the time, however, would presumably enable it to use the facilities of the Permanent Court of Arbitration provided, at any rate, it were willing to act through Great Britain. Whether it would do this is a matter of some doubt.

ROOT-BRYCE TREATY, 1908

Until after the War, however, Canadian disputes with the United States were officially treated as disputes between the latter country and Great Britain, and the important North Atlantic Fisheries case of 1909–1910 was arbitrated at The Hague by arbiters selected from the Court. The submission followed upon the conclusion, in 1908, of the first general arbitration treaty between Great Britain and the United States. That treaty obliged the parties to refer to the Permanent Court of Arbitration differences

of a legal nature or relating to the interpretation of treaties . . . provided, nevertheless, that they do not affect the vital interests, the independence, or the honour of the two Contracting States, and do not concern the interests of third Parties.[6]

5. Sir Charles Fitzpatrick, Chief Justice of Canada, one of the arbiters in the North Atlantic Fisheries case, was a member of the Court by appointment of Great Britain.

6. Article I. For text, see *Treaties and Agreements*, pp. 297–298.

It was also explicitly agreed that the parties should in every case conclude a *compromis* before appealing to the Court.

The Arbitration Convention above referred to was signed at Washington on April 4, 1908; and on the same day an elaborate *compromis*[7] for the submission of the fisheries questions was signed in the same capital. This *compromis* refers in its fourth and fifth articles to the revised Convention for the Settlement of International Disputes concluded at The Hague in 1909, although Great Britain, unlike the United States, has not ratified the revision. There is a similar reference in Article 10 of the Boundary Waters Treaty of 1909.[8] But of course there is nothing to prevent two States from regulating their relations in accordance with the provisions of any treaty, regardless of whether they are parties. In doing so, they are simply adopting *pro tanto* such provisions as part of their own treaty. They would not, of course, be at liberty to use any organ set up by other States, unless the statute of such organ specifically permits non-parties to do so. In this case however, Great Britain and the United States were both participants, under the convention of 1899, in the creation of the Permanent Court of Arbitration. The new convention of 1907 did not deprive the parties to the old of their privileges.

The convention of 1908 was concluded for five years only, but was renewed for similar periods in 1913, 1918, and 1923. Overtures for its further renewal without the now old-fashioned reservation of vital interest, independence, and honor, were made by the State Department in 1927, but the British Government failed to act, with the result that there is at present no general arbitration treaty between Great Britain and the United States, unless the Hague convention of 1899, which, as we have seen, sets up machinery and a regulation for procedure but imposes no obligation to arbitrate, can be so regarded. Nor is there any agreement between the United States and Canada binding these two countries to a general submission of their differences to arbitration.

There are, it is true, two treaties which, with reservations, oblige us not to go to war. The first of these is the Bryan Treaty of 1914, and the second is the Pact of Paris, 1928. A little examination

7. *Treatises and Agreements,* pp. 319–324.   8. *Ibid.,* p. 317.

shows, however, that these agreements are by no means a conclusive guaranty of peaceful settlement.

BRYAN TREATY, 1914

UNDER the Bryan Treaty of 1914,[9] Great Britain and the United States agree, "when diplomatic methods of adjustment have failed," to refer disputes, "of every nature whatsoever, other than disputes the settlement of which is provided for and, in fact, achieved under existing agreements" to a permanent international commission for investigation and report. The report is to be completed within one year after investigation officially begins, and the parties reserve complete liberty of action after it has been submitted to them.

The essence of the arrangement is contained in the last clause of Article I, where the parties undertake not to declare war or begin hostilities before the commission has reported. There is no obligation whatever to accept the report as settlement, the sole purpose being to guard against the outbreak of hostilities in immediate response to real or imagined provocation.

The Dominions were included in the sphere of operation of this agreement, and Great Britain reserved the liberty, if a dispute mainly affects one of them, to substitute for the regular British member of the commission a person representing the Dominion so affected.

The Permanent International Commission consists of five persons, one chosen by each of the contracting parties from its own nationals, one chosen by each of them from some third country, and a fifth, selected by agreement between the two Governments, not a national of either party. It was duly set up, but thus far no occasion for recourse to it has arisen. Since it is to come into operation only in disputes not settled under other agreements, and then only after diplomatic methods have failed, it must be regarded as a last resort of peace. The fact that no need has yet been felt to invoke what is essentially a provision for cases of extreme difficulty is, therefore, a matter for gratification rather than surprise. We may, however, question the wisdom of permitting long-standing vacancies in the commission's membership, as in fact has happened. If the institution

9. *Ibid.*, pp. 463–464.

is worth keeping alive, it should be kept in form for immediate operation. The history of peaceful settlement shows all too clearly the inferior efficacy of commissions and tribunals manned after a dispute has reached the stage of popular apprehension or excitement.

PACT OF PARIS, 1928

ARTICLE II of the much-trumpeted treaty signed at Paris on August 27, 1928, sets out the undertaking that "the settlement or solution of all disputes or conflicts of whatsoever nature or of whatever origin they may be, which may arise among them, shall never be sought, except by pacific means." Canada and the United States were two of the fifteen original signatories of this "Pact of Paris," which has since been adhered to by most of the world's States.

Article II, in spite of its purely negative form, means, if anything, that the parties have bound themselves to employ conciliation and arbitration, rather than war, for the settlement of their differences. But the treaty sets up no organization for these purposes, leaving its signatories free to employ such diplomatic or juridical means as they please. Moreover, the preliminary negotiations, as well as the parliamentary discussions between signature and ratification, consecrate such scope to the exception of self-defense and leave to the parties such complete discretion in defining that concept, that from the first no reliance could be placed on the Pact of Paris as an instrument of peace.[10] Since 1928, the world has become bitterly accustomed to seeing it flouted.

BOUNDARY WATERS TREATY, 1909

THE nearest approach to a general treaty of arbitration now in force between the United States and Canada is the Boundary Waters Treaty of 1909. A brief account of the provisions of this treaty, as well as of the powers, duties, and achievements of the International Joint Commission which it established, has already been given in these pages.[11] What remains to be done is to indicate the limitations

10. See, for example, Mandelstam, *L'Interpretation du pacte Briand-Kellogg par les gouvernements et les parlements des états signataires* (Paris, 1934).

11. Above, pp. 51–59.

which narrow down the functions of the commission far below the measure of competence popularly assigned to it.

The sole compulsory jurisdiction of the International Joint Commission is over the diversion and obstruction of boundary waters, and new uses affecting their natural level or flow. Its powers under Article IX (which provides for the reference on the request of either the American or the Canadian Government of any "other questions or matters of difference . . . involving the rights, obligations, or interests of either contracting party in relation to the other or to the inhabitants of the other, along the common frontier") are merely to examine and report; and it is explicitly declared that reports under this article are not to be regarded as decisions and are in no way to have the character of arbitral awards.

Article IX, though it imposes no obligation of compliance with the commission's findings, has been invoked with some frequency; and in fact those findings have been loyally carried into effect.[12] There is some danger, however, that its potential usefulness may be curtailed by an interpretation which would make investigation and report dependent on the concurrence of both Governments.[13] I would submit that there is no justification in the text for such construction, and that final acceptance of the opinion to that effect expressed by Mr. Tawney, one of the American Commissioners, in the Rainy River hearings, would be a lamentable departure from the intention of the negotiators of the treaty.

The narrowness of the field in which the commission exercises a mandatory function is emphasized by the restrictive meaning imposed on the term "boundary waters" by the Preliminary Article and Article I read together. A question often asked in the debates on the Chicago diversion was why this prolonged dispute should not have been dealt with by a body set up for matters of this very type. The two articles cited, however, make it fairly clear that Lake Michigan was designedly abstracted from the powers of the International Joint Commission. As for investigation and report, the only questions which may be referred for this purpose are such as

12. Exception must be made of the report on the improvement for navigation of the St. Lawrence River between Lake Ontario and Montreal. The treaty finally drawn up in 1932 has not yet been ratified.

13. See Chacko, *op. cit.*, pp. 241 *seq.*

arise along the common frontier; and even then compliance with the report drawn up is entirely optional.

Turning to arbitration properly so called, we find this provided for in an article which is broader in its scope than any other in the Boundary Waters Treaty, but which has never yet been resorted to. In Article X, it is agreed that any question or matters of difference may be referred to the commission for decision. There is no limitation here as to the nature or geographical origin of the dispute; but it is explicitly laid down that reference under this article can only be by consent of both parties in each individual case, the United States acting with the advice and consent of the Senate, His Majesty's Government with the consent of the Governor General of Canada in Council. Upon any matter so submitted, the commission is empowered to decide by a majority. In the event of equal division, its duty is to report the differing conclusions to both Governments, whereupon the dispute is to be referred for decision to an umpire chosen in accordance with the procedure set out in Article 45 of the Hague Convention of 1907 for the Pacific Settlement of International Disputes.

The effect of this article is merely to recognize the International Joint Commission as a body which the parties may use for arbitral purpose if both are simultaneously so inclined. Reference by joint consent would take the form of a *compromis* which might explicitly restrict the function and powers of the commission in respect of the dispute submitted.[14] The treaty, therefore, imposes no obligation to arbitrate.

The Boundary Waters Treaty was concluded for five years and made terminable, after that period, by twelve months' notice from either side.[15] The quinquennium expired on May 5, 1915, and the arrangement therefore depends now for its survival on the absence of the specified notice. But the International Joint Commission has made such a place for itself in the relations of the United States and Canada that its prospect of permanency is high.

It is doubtful whether any use will ever be made of Article X. The International Joint Commission had shown admirable competence in dealing with questions of a technical nature relating to water levels

14. See Article X, first paragraph *in fine*.
15. Article 14, *Treaties and Agreements,* p. 318.

and the measures necessary to preserve them against unreasonable obstruction or diversion. But it can scarcely be said to have been manned with a view to the legal solution of disputes which diplomacy has proved incapable of settling. There is indeed a fairly obvious tendency to treat membership in the commission as a suitable reward for political services, a criterion of selection not entirely calculated to guarantee that impartiality, training, and knowledge required for the objective adjudication of burning issues.

PECUNIARY CLAIMS AGREEMENT, 1910

A LARGE number of claims arising out of alleged wrongs to Canadians at the hands of American citizens and to American citizens at the hands of Canadians have been disposed of by two pecuniary claims tribunals, one appointed under a convention of 1853, and the other under an agreement of 1910.[16] Both the constitutive treaties were between the United States and the British Empire as a whole; but the bulk of the work done by the second tribunal had reference to Canada, and one of its remarkable features was the antiquity of some of the cases handled. The *Lord Nelson* and the case of the Cayuga Indians had their origin in the War of 1812. But though the Agreement of 1910 reached a long way back, it did not reach forward at all. That is to say that it contemplated only claims outstanding in 1910. Moreover, any claim so outstanding but not presented by one party to the other within four months after the confirmation of the Agreement of 1910 (a confirmation which took place by exchange of notes on April 26, 1912) is forever barred by explicit provision in Article II.

The tribunal completed its first schedule of claims in 1926, but it may conceivably be reconvened, without a new treaty, to deal with a number of cases presented by the Governments within the time prescribed but not yet grouped in an accepted schedule. It cannot, however, be resorted to for any new disputes, unless the signatories make specific agreement to that effect. One such agreement is contained in the fourth article of the Convention respecting the Regulation of the Liquor Traffic concluded in 1924. It is there provided

16. For the work of the first, see above, pp. 26–28; of the second, above, pp. 63–68.

that if the two persons nominated by the contracting parties, as Chief Justice Duff and Mr. Justice Van Devanter were nominated to deal with the *I'm Alone* controversy, fail to achieve a joint report, the claim shall be referred to the

Claims Commission established under . . . the Agreement . . . signed at Washington, 1910, but the claim shall not, before submission to the tribunal, require to be included in a schedule of claims confirmed in the manner therein provided.

In spite of the repeal of the legislation prohibiting the sale of alcoholic liquors in the United States, legislation which was the *raison d'être* of the convention of 1924, that convention, though terminable after fifteen months on the initiative of either party,[17] is still in force. It may therefore be held that, whether or not the second list of pecuniary claims is ever constituted a schedule and submitted to the tribunal established for that purpose by the Agreement of 1910, the provisions of Article 4 of the liquor convention cited in the preceding paragraph will, so long as they are in force, keep that agreement alive.

A short summary will now reveal the deficiencies of Canadian-American machinery for the adjudication of disputes. The Hague convention of 1899, and the revising convention of 1907 to which Great Britain and the Dominions are not parties, merely provide an organization which can be used if States decide to arbitrate. The general arbitration treaty of 1908, with its reservations of vital interests, national honor, and independence, came to an end through failure of renewal in 1928. The Boundary Waters Treaty of 1909 sets up a body, the International Joint Commission, whose compulsory jurisdiction is restricted to diversion, obstruction, and new uses of boundary waters, whose function of investigation extends only to questions arising along the common frontier, and whose arbitral function can come into play only by the special consent of the two Governments. The Bryan Treaty of 1914 prohibits war over any dispute before investigation by a Permanent International Commission has been completed, but leaves the parties free to take what action they please when that commission has submitted its report. The Pact of Paris, though it purports to outlaw war in general and

17. Article 5, *Treaties and Agreements*, p. 511.

prohibits the settlement of any difference by other than peaceful means, makes no positive provision for adjudication and, moreover, is stultified by reservations which except areas of special interest and embody an illimitable concept of self-defense.

Thus, the documents furnish nothing approaching a universal assurance that injuries between Canada and the United States will find reasonably prompt and impartial settlement. Many conflicts might occur for which, on examination, no mutual obligation to proceed to adjudication would be found to exist. The remedy for this situation is of the simplest. A treaty of two short articles would fill all the existing gaps. The first article would oblige each party, on application from the other, to submit all disputes to judicial settlement. The second would designate some existing body to adjudicate, or would provide for a new standing tribunal to deal with all cases not clearly covered by one or another of our present arrangements. It is a reason for some wonder that two countries so amicably disposed as Canada and the United States should not have such an "all-in" arbitral agreement. Instead we depend, or so it would appear, upon the automatic continuance of that friendship which it is the precise purpose of arbitration treaties to safeguard.

The disadvantages, not to say dangers, of such dependence may be illustrated from the history of a long-standing cause of irritation in Canada against her neighbor. I refer to the diversion of water from Lake Michigan by the Chicago Sanitary District. This has been mentioned once or twice in passing, but the successive stages of the dispute, and the unsatisfactory efforts to dispose of it, argue so strongly for arbitration that they must receive fuller attention.

Permission to divert water from Lake Michigan was first granted to the Chicago Sanitary District in 1899 by the United States Secretary of War in exercise of his jurisdiction over navigable waterways. The amount authorized, 5,000 cubic feet per second, was in 1901 reduced to 4,167 cubic feet. Successive applications for large increases in this diversion were refused by the same authority. On the occasion of one of these applications, in 1912, the Canadian Government lodged a protest through the British Ambassador at Washington, and the reasons given by Mr. Stimson, then Secretary of War, for rejecting Chicago's demand are of especial interest. He declared that the question was both national and international. The

Boundary Waters Treaty gave citizens of both countries equal rights of navigation in the Great Lakes and connecting rivers. Article VIII, urged by the applicants as giving preference to sanitary and domestic purposes over navigation, applied only to future cases before the International Joint Commission and contemplated only ordinary use for these purposes. It would be contrary to national policy to give preference to extraordinary use substantially injuring navigation. The Canadian Government regarded the proposed diversion as affecting material interests of the Dominion. Then follows a memorable passage:

The establishment by formal treaty between the two countries, of a tribunal to decide just such questions seems to me to afford an additional reason against the assumption of jurisdiction to decide the question by an administrative officer of one of those countries.

At this time and later, Canada insisted that the diversion was in fact greatly in excess of the authorized 4,167 cubic feet per second, and was being increased by new canal construction. Any diversion, she maintained, which prejudicially affected navigation of the Great Lakes invaded her rights under the Ashburton-Webster Treaty of 1842 (Article 7) and the Boundary Waters Treaty of 1909 (Article I), and, quite apart from such treaties, was a violation of recognized principles of international law. The practical effect would be to render useless the construction of canals and harbors which had cost the Canadian people two hundred million dollars. Her protests were renewed in 1916, 1921, 1923, and 1924.[18]

Meanwhile the Sanitary District, without permission, had increased the drain on Lake Michigan up to and over 10,000 cubic feet per second. This amount, Mr. Stimson had stated in 1913, would substantially diminish the navigable capacity of the Great Lakes and their connecting rivers. In 1923, the Government of the United States was granted an injunction by the United States District Court restraining Chicago from taking off more than 4,167 cubic feet. Time was allowed, however, for appeal to the Supreme Court, and appeal was duly entered. From that date until 1933, litigation on the matter continued in the Supreme Court, with refer-

18. For an official account of the whole matter up to 1923, see *Sessional Papers,* Canada, No. 180.

ences to special masters, rehearings, and complaints against Chicago from such riparian states as Michigan, Minnesota, Ohio, and Wisconsin. Throughout this period Canadian discontent was growing. Marine associations and chambers of commerce lodged vigorous protests at Ottawa, the press of Ontario and Quebec made constant allusion to the "Chicago Water Steal," and loud dissatisfaction was expressed up and down the Dominion at the Government's unwillingness or inability to take any effective steps to arrest a practice which, it was alleged, threatened ruin to navigation interests along the Canadian border. In 1930 the Supreme Court ordered the Sanitary District of Chicago to reduce the drainage to 6,500 cubic feet per second by July 1, 1930, to 5,000 cubic feet by December 31, 1935, and to 1,500 cubic feet by December 31, 1938.[19] Riparian states complained in 1932 that this order was not being complied with, and the Supreme Court ordered the State of Illinois to provide money for the completion of sewage works which would permit the specified reduction.[20]

The Canadian Government, which had hitherto allowed American Federal and state authorities to fight the battle, got what looked like a chance of effective action in 1932, when the treaty for the improvement of the international portion of the St. Lawrence River was drawn up. On the ground that it would be folly to proceed with costly development which might be rendered fruitless at any time by unauthorized drainage, it secured the inclusion in the draft treaty of an article requiring the Chicago diversion to be reduced to the quantity specified in the Supreme Court's order of 1930. Any dispute over proposals that might be made by the United States to increase this quantity for emergency purposes was to be referred to an arbitral tribunal of three, one member appointed by the United States, one by Canada, and the chairman to be selected by agreement between the Governments. But this treaty has never been ratified.

Now it may be argued that an obligation to arbitrate would have been useless in this case, because the facts showed complete inability on the part of the American Federal authority to control the con-

19. Supreme Court, April 21, 1930, 74 *Law Ed.* 1124.
20. Supreme Court, May 22, 1933, 77 *Law Ed.* 1292.

duct of a municipal subdivision. That point is, however, not proven. In spite of Mr. Stimson's reasoning in 1912, the matter has been somewhat arrogantly treated as a domestic one. It has been denied by the interested parties that the Boundary Waters Treaty has any application, since Lake Michigan is not within the definition of boundary waters. If there had been a clear international duty the Federal Government could hardly have failed to make more effective efforts at restraint, and the reference to the Supreme Court, with the consequent delays, would probably have been unnecessary. There is some reason for believing even now that the orders of the Supreme Court, under the vigilant pressure of the riparian States, will be literally enforced. But the Canadian Government showed its appreciation of the advantage which it would gain from the right to demand arbitration, rather than being forced to depend upon agencies internal to the United States, when it had the arbitral provisions inserted in Article 8 of the draft treaty for the development of the St. Lawrence Waterway.

Piecemeal arrangement for arbitration, such as that contained in the article just cited and in Article 4 of the 1924 liquor convention, is better than no arrangement at all; but it is not enough. It leaves the door too widely ajar for disputes that may sour relations to the danger point before *ad hoc* provision can be made for settlement. Nor is the special tribunal to which such particular agreements incline the best instrumentality for rational adjudication. The business of choosing commissioners may be greatly complicated and even unduly influenced by the passions aroused by the conflict in process. No more cogent illustration of this danger could be found than the history of the Alaskan boundary case. The standing tribunal, whether its jurisdiction be general or limited to a specified class of disputes, offers invaluable advantages. It is detached from the particular issue, it has the opportunity to develop a consistent jurisprudence, it can inspire a habit of public confidence. This is not to deny that notable successes have been achieved by *ad hoc* tribunals. The preceding pages bear ample witness to the power of judicial detachment over the most unruly problems. But when no regular and permanent organ exists, there is always a more or less prolonged period of public uncertainty either as to whether a given dispute will be referred to arbitration or as to whether a suitable commission will be set up; and sometimes both uncertainties concur. Such uncertainty means anxiety, and anxiety aggravates the animosity which inevitably accompanies international conflicts of interest.

Canadian-American relations benefited greatly from the achievements of the two pecuniary claims tribunals whose work has been described in these pages. These bodies were established to deal with accumulations of disputes, and most readers of their records will agree that they contrived on the whole to render substantial justice. But many of the claims dealt with were of such long standing that dependable evidence was unprocurable and the assessment of due compensation rendered almost impossible by fundamental changes in circumstances. What escape is there from the conclusion that there ought to be a standing court to which matters of this sort would be referred *as they arise*, not a hundred years after the events?

In conclusion it should be pointed out that a small country involved in a dispute with one having twelve times its population may be expected to harbor some doubt as to whether it will obtain justice. The result is an irritated state of mind which produces recrimination and a progressive accumulation of bad feeling. Popular knowledge that a regular judicial procedure is provided for every conflict that may occur would, it is not unreasonable to hope, prevent that working up of general indignation which imperils the friendly relations of States and obstructs rational collaboration in the prosecution of their common interests.

CHAPTER VIII

CONCLUSION

In the long period which we have covered in this survey of Canadian-American disputes and their settlement, the practice of arbitration among other nations has increased in something like geometric progression. A century and a half ago it was a rare alternative to war; now it has so truly become the normal mode of adjusting international differences, that a State which resorts to force without a sincere attempt at peaceful adjudication is regarded as a violator of the moral, if not the legal, code of nations. The observation is a commonplace which is repeated here only because the revolutionary change which it signifies in the feelings of peoples toward one another is ignored alike by the enemies and the friends of international organization.

The part played in this change by the British Empire and the United States, through the submission of disputes regarding their interests in North America to tribunals whose proceedings were sometimes conducted with stately ceremony and vast publicity, is obvious to students of history and has been too often noticed to require further elaboration here. Curiously enough, though it was these two great States which revived arbitration in the modern world, they were not the first to conclude a treaty for the submission of future disputes as opposed to quarrels already in progress. The honor for this long step in the safeguarding of peace by attacking the causes of war near their source falls to Great Britain and France.

The Anglo-French Treaty of 1903, providing for arbitration of all matters not affecting "national honour or vital interests" was the precursor of a network of similar agreements, many of which preceded by several years our Root-Bryce Treaty of 1908. The fact that the parties to these treaties could refuse to submit any dispute whatever simply because it was important to them should not blind our eyes to the reality of the progress marked by their conclusion. The results actually achieved under their provisions, if we take only the British-American record analyzed in the previous chapters of this essay, are their abundant justification.

The exception of "vital interest and national honour" is now happily old-fashioned. There remains, however, one flaw in the generality of most recent arrangements for the adjudication of disputes by permanent or *ad hoc* tribunals. That is the limitation to disputes of a legal or justiciable nature. The purpose of this restriction is to reserve freedom of action in the vague category of so called "political" disputes. But as there never has been anything approaching an agreed limitative definition of "political dispute," it remains possible for the parties to withhold from arbitration any given difference simply by insisting that it falls within an entirely arbitrary classification.

If there is any substance in the distinction, it lies only in the fact that disputes may and do arise which cannot be permanently and equitably disposed of by the application of positive, concrete rules of law. They can be settled, technically speaking, by recourse to the principle that States have a right to do all that is not forbidden by existing international law. They are the sort of case in which a municipal court applies its interpretation of the existing law with express regret and commends the sufferer to the mercies of the legislature. As there is not yet any formal and organized legislature with authority over States, the contention is that questions of this nature, calling for a dynamic rather than a static law of nations, must for the present be kept within the unqualified sovereignty of the State.

There are of course those who argue that the distinction between "legal" and "political" disputes, even so limited, assumes a static quality in international law which that much maligned system does not in fact possess. For such theorists, international law, even strictly so called, includes those general principles of justice to which no body of concrete rules can ever be more than an approximation. The system, in other words, is already dynamic in that it is the duty of the international judge to create a new rule, where the old one, or the want of one, works a violation of prevailing standards of justice and equity.

There is now a growing inclination so to extend the function of the judge in municipal law, and it may be that we shall in future reach such an ideal in the international sphere. But in present prac-tice, the dominant tendency is to restrict the law of nations to a body of rules, very difficult to specify, which have received "general consent." That being so, progressive jurists in Europe are devoting much effort to a movement for the establishment of an international court of equity, or alternatively for the expansion of the competence of existing tribunals by empowering them to pronounce judgment *ex aequo et bono*. This would furnish the society of nations with a body or bodies explicitly authorized to deal with disputes properly classified as "political," and to impose settlement not commanded by any existing specific rule. Thus at one stroke a remedy would be pro-vided for the sparsity of the accepted law and the lack of an inter-national legislature to fill lacunae and repeal the obsolete.

In this effort they are finding valuable assistance in the history of English equity and in the recourse of British-American arbitral courts and commissions to ideas of equity no less broad and effica-cious than those which inspired the early chancellors and served as a corrective to the rigidity of the common law.[1] The reader who has been patient enough to follow us through the preceding chapters will probably draw two conclusions: the first, that for the purposes of British-American arbitration no special court is required to bring a liberal and living equity to bear upon problems for which law nar-rowly interpreted would provide no lasting solution; the second, that the power to go outside the rules of law strictly so called in order to reach a just decision does indeed add greatly to the chances of rational settlement. It may well be that we have here the best in-strument for the much needed development of international law.

The remarkable success of arbitration between Canada and the United States is due to the fact that these two countries have suffi-cient respect for judicial methods and their common legal tradition to endow their joint tribunals with the power of deciding according

1. See, for example, Friedmann, *The Contribution of English Equity to the Idea of an International Equity Tribunal;* Habicht, *The Power of the International Judge To Give a Decision* ex aequo et bono; Schwarzenberger, *William Ladd: An Examination of an American Proposal for an Interna-tional Equity Tribunal.* These three short monographs were published in 1935 by the New Commonwealth Institute, London. Dr. Habicht, *op. cit.,* pp. 64–65, makes use of the award in the Cayuga Indian claims dealt with above, pp. 91–92 and 109–110.

to "law and equity," and then to accept, in the main with no more
discontent than the losing litigant may be expected to manifest, a
liberal interpretation by the arbiters of what constitutes equity in
the matter at issue. They have even, in the two important cases of
the Behring Sea and Atlantic fisheries, given something like a power
of legislation to their chosen arbiters. Such indeed is their faith in
the possibility of settlement by judicial means, that they have
neglected to mantain general provision in advance, allowing their
arbitral machinery to fall into disrepair, and counting upon *ad hoc*
arrangements as each dispute presents itself.

The detached student, realizing what has happened, finds difficulty in giving any effective warning. He cannot hold over his fellow North Americans an imminent peril of war, for his knowledge of
history leads him on the whole to share the less documented assurance of the politician. The long habit of peaceful settlement has
simply driven out of the minds of these two peoples the thought of
war as a mode of vindicating their rights against one another, and it
is no part of the business of the political theorist to awaken a false
sense of alarm in order to bring about the reform of what are to him
obvious defects in the institutions destined for their common use. It
is his business, however, to point out these defects and to suggest
their cure. For his work is not finished with the elimination of war.
Friction, suspicion, discontent, though they may always stop short
of violence, have their wasteful effects in practice. They impede the
business of getting the best for human use out of the resources available where the exploitation of those resources needs any measure of
joint regulation. No one who reads the legislative debates upon business under negotiation between the United States and Canada can
fail to observe how resentments born in other spheres of common
concern engender or reënforce opposition to progress in the matter
in hand. For specific illustration we need go no farther afield than
the murky history of the proposals to improve navigation and increase power development in the St. Lawrence waterways. There is
still sufficient childish distrust between Canadians and Americans to
prevent, especially when it is worked upon by selfish vested interests,
the calmly reasoned examination of projects for enhancing our common welfare. The view has been expressed in these pages that a firm
agreement, without reservations, to submit all differences to arbitra-

tion by a standing tribunal of the best judicial talent in both countries, would go far to remove that fear of injustice which causes recurrent and sometimes prolonged spasms of popular agitation over
real or imaginary injuries. These agitations keep alive the prejudice
over which all new plans of collaborative activity have to fight their
way.

Where special technical qualifications are needed for handling
business of specific types, as for example in the regulation of water
levels and the use of the fisheries, special provision should continue
to be made in the agreements which must from time to time be concluded or revised for the adjudication of claims. But in the wide inter-
stices between such special fields there will continue to be room for un-
predictable clashes of alleged rights and liberties. To deal with these,
we need no such duplication of courts of law and courts of equity as
is being urged by the European publicists cited above. We have not
suffered from any inability on the part of our arbitral agencies to
find a principle of settlement. Experience shows that our judges are
not likely to be defeated in their search for a reasonable solution by
the sparsity or fixity of the rules of international law. Our dis-
satisfactions have been occasioned by improper modes of constitut-
ing *ad hoc* tribunals and the choice of arbiters already committed to
a particular view of the case, or by the fact that a dispute falls
through some loophole in arrangements apparently designed to dispose of it. Both of these vices would be cured by the establishment of
a permanent court of general jurisdiction manned with competent
and independent judges.

INDEX